MAKER

LIVE SUSTAINABLY!

COMICS

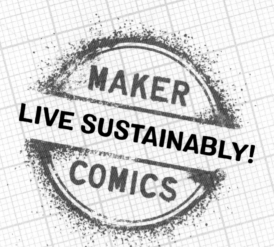

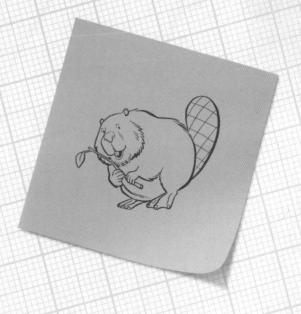

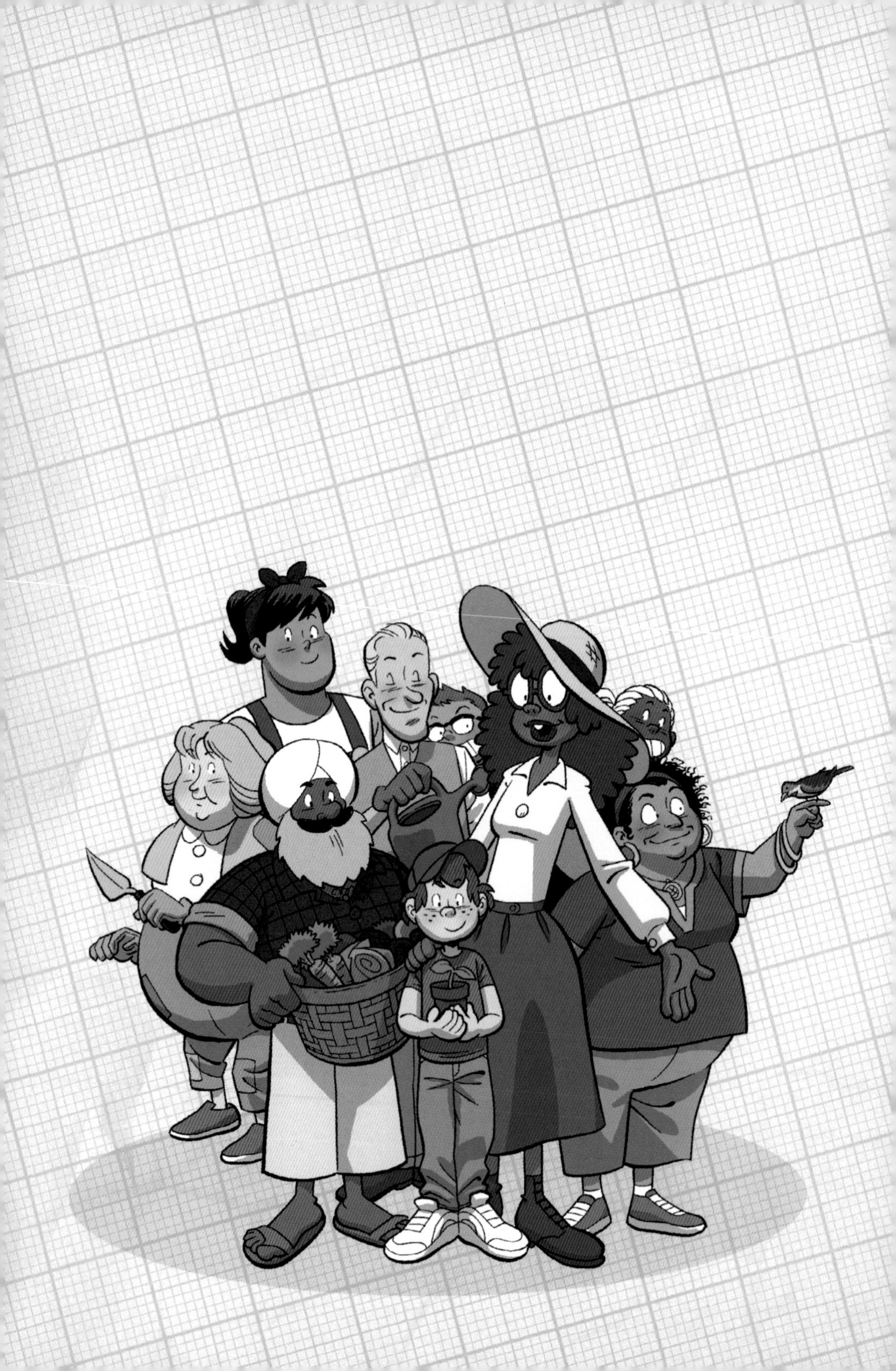

LIVE SUSTAINABLY!

Written by Angela Boyle
Art by Les McClaine

:01

First Second
New York

You can make many simple changes to live more sustainably, but with a little hard work and elbow grease, you can make an even bigger difference. As long as you do so carefully!

Be sure to pay attention to the safety notes throughout the book. And ask an adult to help you when projects include power tools, sharp knives, the stove, hot wax, and other items that could potentially cause injury.

You and your adult should wear proper clothing when working on projects. Wear goggles and pants when using power tools. Wear gloves to lower risk for cuts and burns. Wear long sleeves and hats outside to prevent sunburn. And wear proper shoes. Sneakers are fine, boots are better, but no flip-flops. Cover those toes!

If you are working in a community garden or other shared space, be sure to follow any rules that are in place. If something is against the rules, this can be an opportunity to discuss your project with the leaders of the shared space and bring issues of sustainability to the group.

Your local garden center or extension office (soil and wildlife department) can help you with many projects, including making sure your projects don't violate any local ordinances. They can also help you pick native plants when gardening. And they might be able to help you get in contact with sustainability movements in your area.

...Dumbest punishment ever...

For a whole week?!

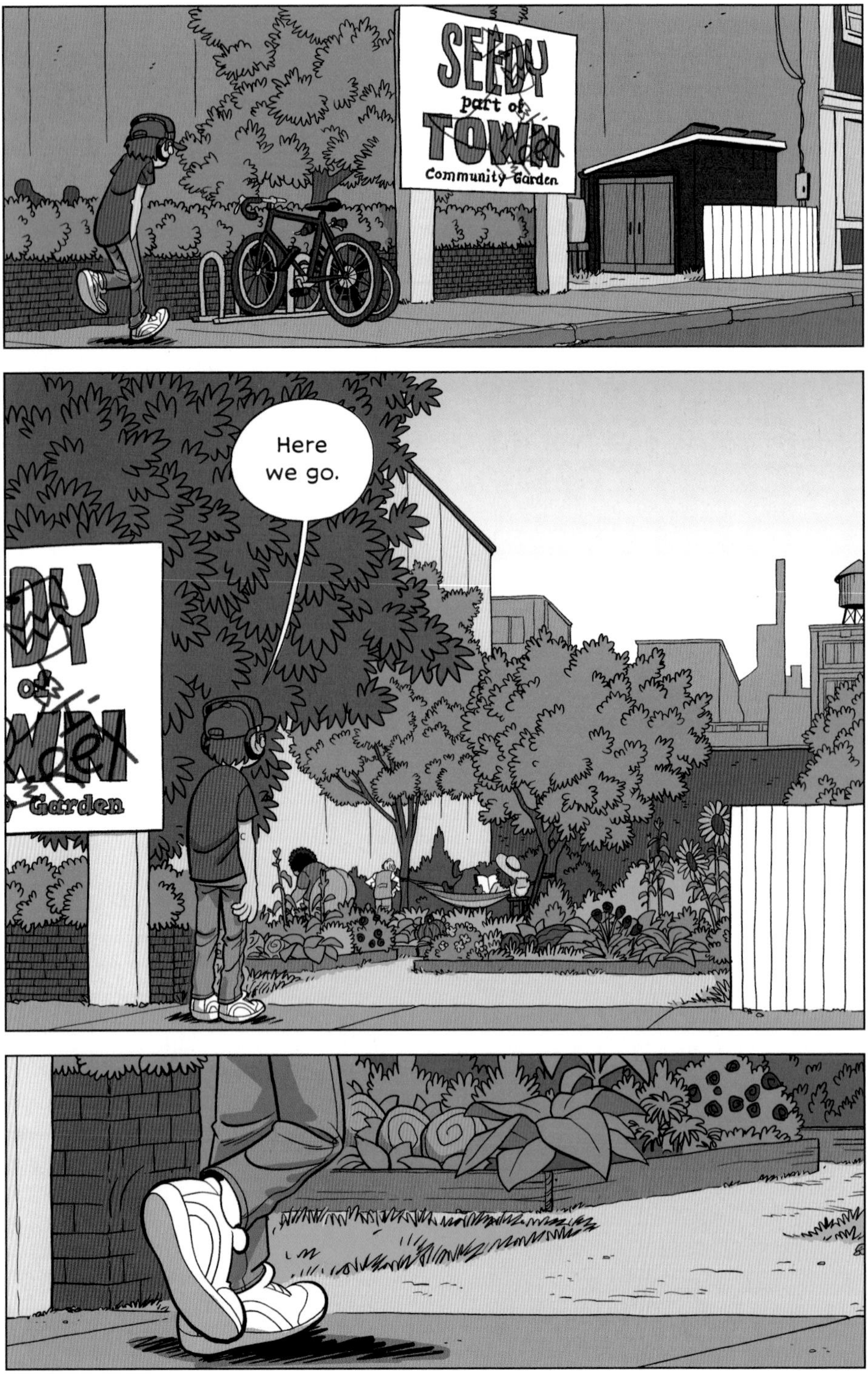
SEEDY
part of
TOWN
Community Garden
Here we go.

Good afternoon, Isaac!

Hi, Aurora.

Glad to see you're excited to lend us a hand.

Would you like a glass of lemonade? Made fresh!

No.

Thanks.

I just want to finish this stupid community service and go home.

3

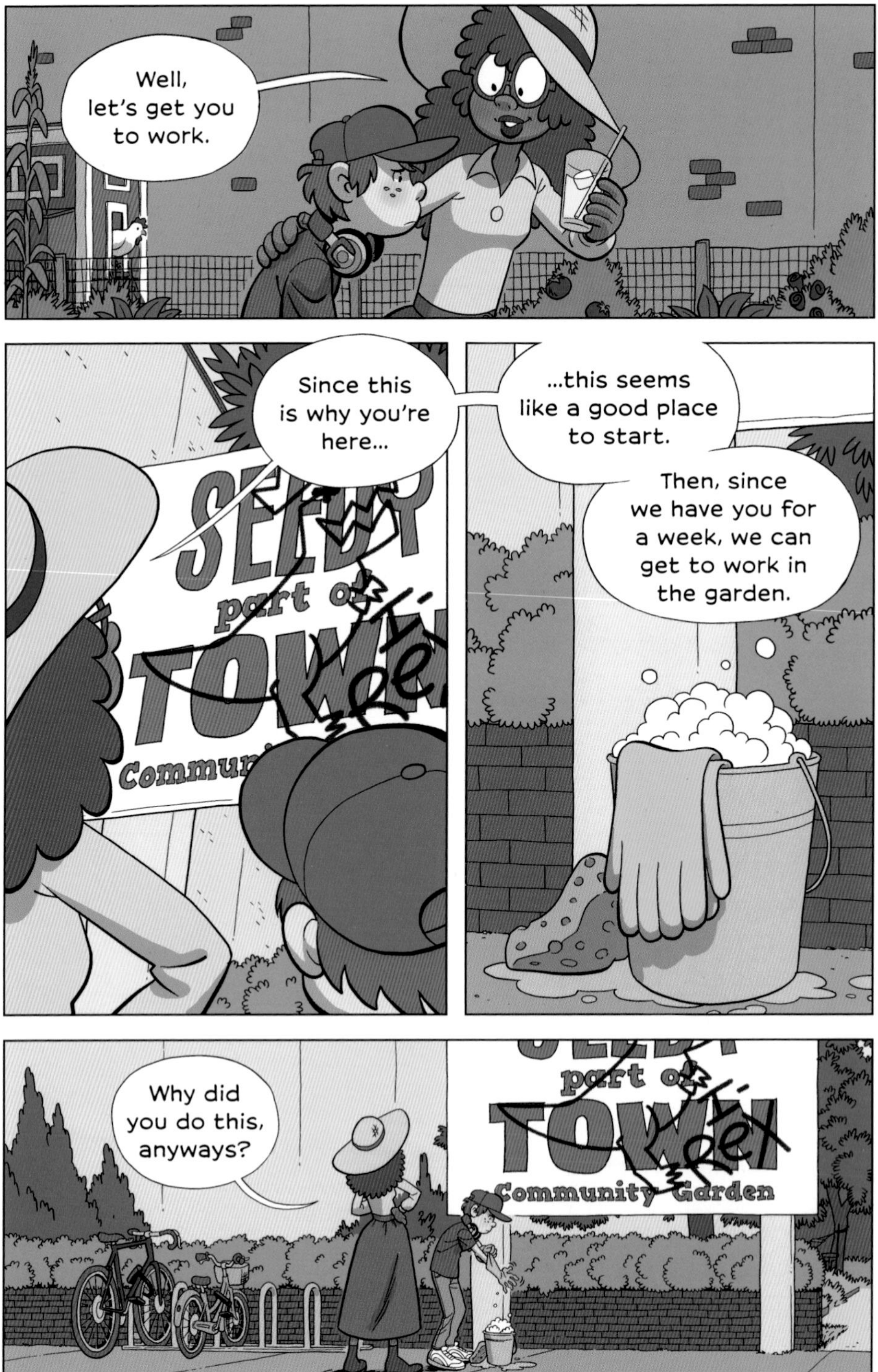
Well, let's get you to work.
Since this is why you're here...
...this seems like a good place to start.
Then, since we have you for a week, we can get to work in the garden.
Why did you do this, anyways?
part of TOWN
Community Garden
REX

I dunno.

Isaac, do you know why community gardens like this are important?

I dunno.

We're working toward a more sustainable future for everyone.

What does that even mean?

5

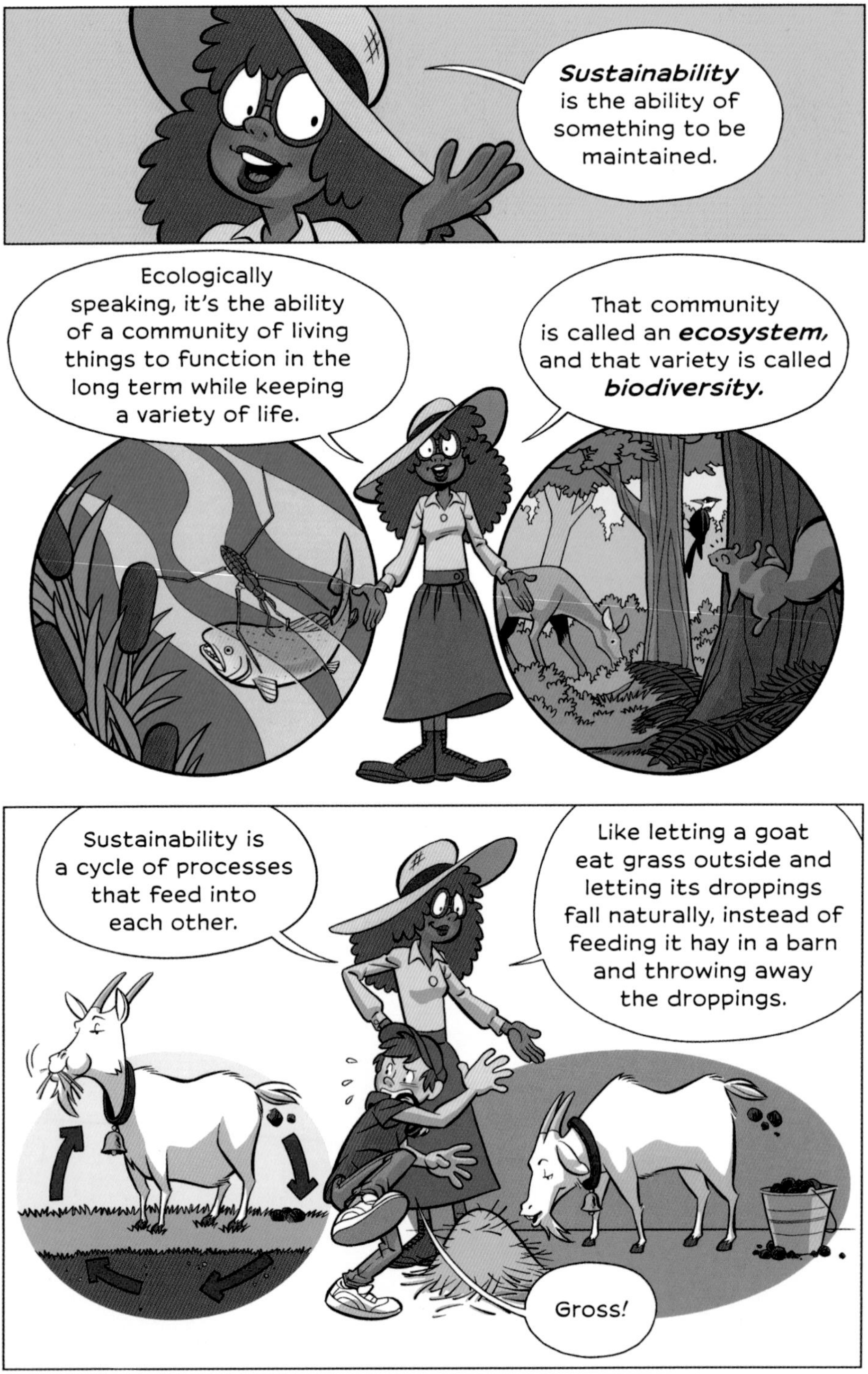
Sustainability is the ability of something to be maintained.
Ecologically speaking, it's the ability of a community of living things to function in the long term while keeping a variety of life.
That community is called an **ecosystem,** and that variety is called **biodiversity.**
Sustainability is a cycle of processes that feed into each other.
Like letting a goat eat grass outside and letting its droppings fall naturally, instead of feeding it hay in a barn and throwing away the droppings.
Gross!

Ha-ha!

Goat poop's not so bad. In this goat cycle, the droppings are fertilizer, a substance added to soil to help fertility, which helps the grass grow.

The droppings are an organic fertilizer. *Organic* simply means no chemical pesticides or fertilizers.

To live sustainably, we have to meet our *basic needs* while creating minimal *waste.* Waste is anything we don't use completely.

So, anything we throw away?

Yes! And to keep our water clean and our air breathable, we need to live within the limits of the available resources.

Otherwise, we'll damage our environment.

What limits? We have everything we need—

phones, clothes, cars.

For the most part, we do. At least in this city, at this time.

But that's not true for everyone.

And these resources can and will run out.

I can't do anything. I'm just a kid. My folks won't even buy me a new cell.

And I really need it!

Everyone can help.

To start, think about actual needs versus wants— what we need to survive and what we want just to make our lives easier.

Basic needs are food, drinking water, shelter, and anything **required to live.**

We must also care for the environment where we get the resources to meet those needs.

Oh, like our antipollution laws to keep our water and air clean and safe.

Right! Sewage treatment plants remove waste and bacteria so we can reuse the water, instead of dumping it.

On the flip side, anything that's not a basic need is a *want.*

Though some wants are very powerful, like a cell.

Or even ice cream.

You think a phone is a want?!

To fill those needs—and wants—sustainably, we should use renewable resources whenever we can.

Renewable?

That means it's naturally replaced. Most of the parts in your cell aren't renewable—we can't grow a new one.

We can only make a certain number of phones before they go extinct?!

Earth is a *closed system,* meaning nothing comes in or out for the most part.* So we have only what is here.

* Meteors come from outside the system. The sun technically comes from off-planet, but it's so reliable and required, it can count as part of the system.

But Earth is bursting with cycles, such as the solar and water cycles. And with life!

Like those goats!

Exactly!

Things that grow can be used sustainably, making them renewable resources.

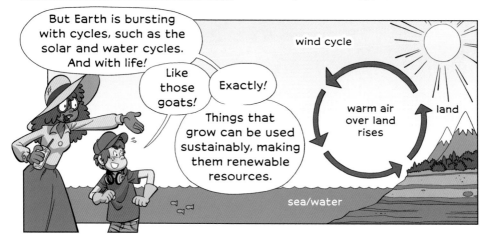

wind cycle

warm air over land rises

land

sea/water

Like the life cycle?

Yeah, that one's easy to see because we are living it. All things are born, grow, reproduce, and die. But that death is often life-giving to other living things.

Remember, Earth is a closed system. The *solar cycle*—the heat and energy we get from the sun—is the only external input the Earth receives.

And it is incredibly important.

But aren't we blocking the sun with smog and tall buildings?

That's true. We can affect something as powerful as the sun's energy, an important part of life on Earth.

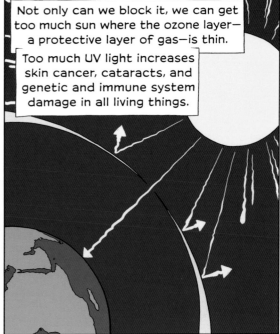

Not only can we block it, we can get too much sun where the ozone layer—a protective layer of gas—is thin.

Too much UV light increases skin cancer, cataracts, and genetic and immune system damage in all living things.

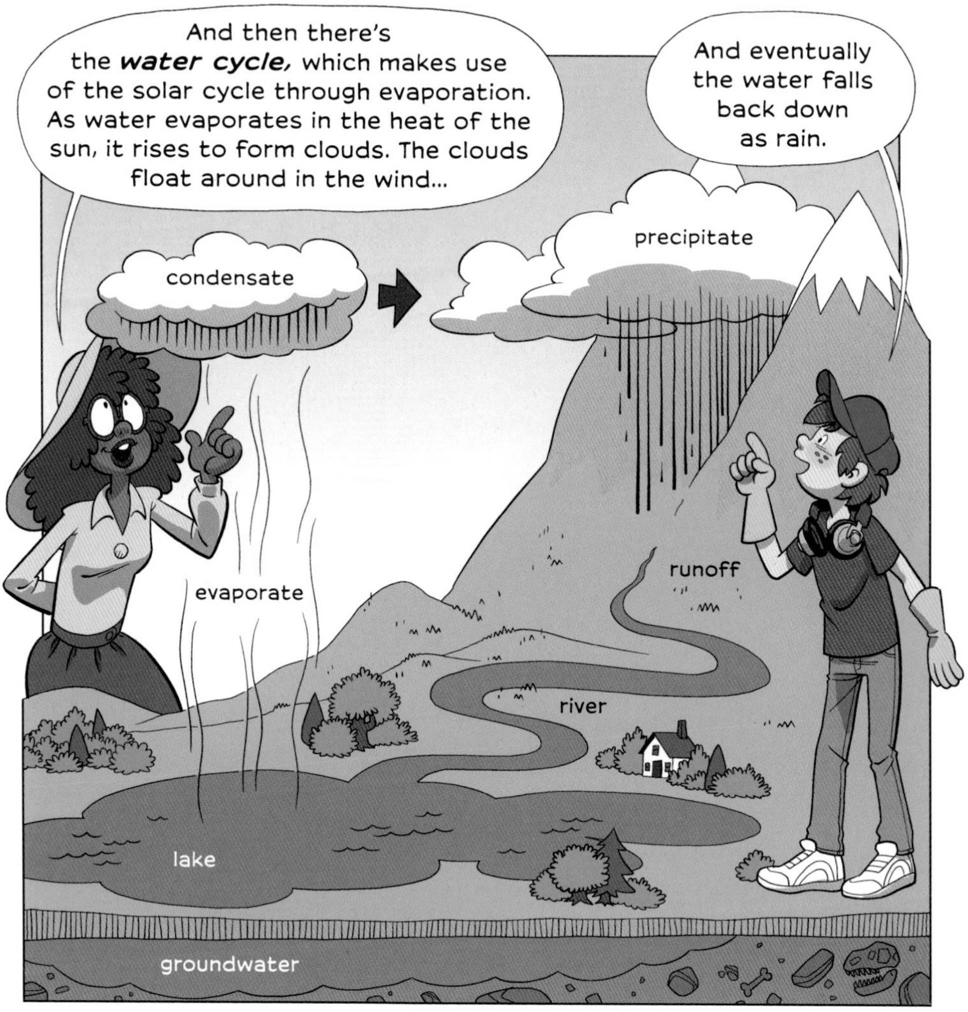
And then there's the ***water cycle,*** which makes use of the solar cycle through evaporation. As water evaporates in the heat of the sun, it rises to form clouds. The clouds float around in the wind...
And eventually the water falls back down as rain.
condensate
precipitate
evaporate
runoff
river
lake
groundwater

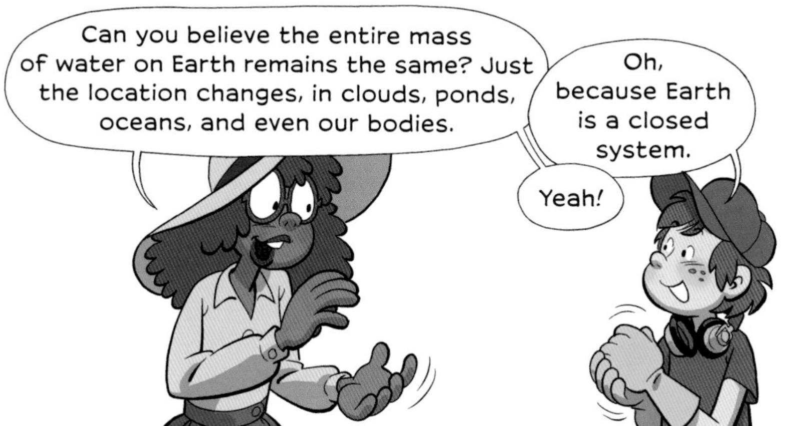
Can you believe the entire mass of water on Earth remains the same? Just the location changes, in clouds, ponds, oceans, and even our bodies.
Oh, because Earth is a closed system.
Yeah!

The ground might seem like an unchanging lump, but even soil has a cycle, following the yearly cycle of plants that grow in it, as well as a millennia-long cycle of erosion and pressure.

plants

animals

poo

soil

rot

bacteria
insects
fungi

minerals
nutrients

Good soil that grows lots of healthy plants has worms, bugs, bacteria, and fungi.

These cycles are important because the *ecosystems*—living and non-living things in an area—rely upon them. Even this garden is an ecosystem!

monarch
butterfly

milkweed

Tennant Lake's another example. It's an ecosystem in the Puget Sound in western Washington.

Animals, particularly birds, can easily move between different small ecosystems.

Wow! A giant bird!

great blue heron

Even though they can leave, the birds are still important to the ecosystem of Tennant Lake.

I'll bet that big bird could eat these little birds.*

* They will, though it's not their first choice in food.

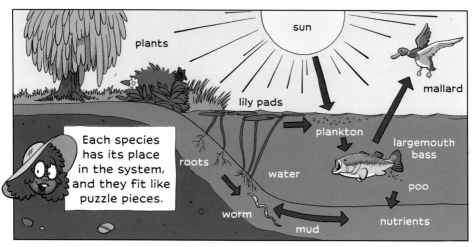

Each species has its place in the system, and they fit like puzzle pieces.

plants

sun

mallard

lily pads

plankton

largemouth bass

roots

water

poo

nutrients

worm

mud

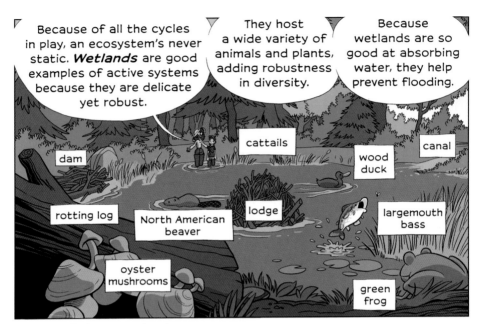

A lot of these wetlands are made by beavers. Many wetlands rely on beaver dams to regulate aboveground water flow.

Humans regulate water using culverts—big metal pipes that allow water to flow where we want it to.

But our culverts are static systems that don't adapt to changing needs like beaver dams do.

Because beavers work on their dams all the time?

Yeah. They are continually making changes based on how much water there is, both as rain and standing water.

Beavers are a **keystone species.** Without them, the ecosystem falls apart. Or we can introduce them to renew it with fresh life.

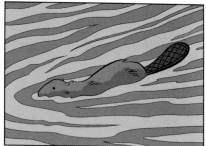

I thought beavers were a nuisance. My uncle complains they flood farms and ruin crops.

They can be a nuisance, flooding where the farmers want to plant.

But they're invaluable in an area that has destructive flooding or summer droughts.

How does that work?

Their dams and canals—the waterways they dig to move logs—create a pond that collects runaway flooding.

doot de doo

The pond also holds water during a drought because of the beavers' vigilant care.

Beavers' work is extra useful because of climate change.

While natural climate change takes place over very long periods—hundreds of thousands of years—our current rate of change has sped up to just a few hundred years, largely from our use of fossil fuels.

Because the overall temperature is increasing, ice that previously held large quantities of water—such as glaciers and the polar ice caps—are melting.

Huh. I guess that water has to go somewhere. But how can you tell the temperature is increasing? Seems fine to me.

We use satellites to measure the ocean temperature. You might not feel the difference, but when Earth's average temperature changes even a few degrees, it affects ecosystems all over the planet.

Islands are flooding, becoming smaller or disappearing, because the oceans are rising when the ice caps and glaciers melt.

the Maldives, Indian Ocean

Local weather is also affected by climate change. The weather changes when air at different temperatures collides. The bigger the difference, the more chaotic and unpredictable the storm.

Like all the gigantic tsunamis and hurricanes? Those are scary. My pen pal in Puerto Rico told me about some storms he's been through.

Exactly. Hurricanes get energy from the heat of the ocean, so as the ocean heats up, the storms become more powerful. Tornadoes are similar but on land, and occur when warm, humid air collides with cold, dry air. Because hot air holds more water than cold, the storms can rain more.

Tsunamis are also caused by underwater earthquakes. Melting ice changes the pressures on the ocean floor, putting strain on earthquake fault lines.

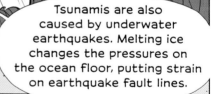

We cause most of this climate change. We aren't maintaining the natural cycles. By disrupting them, we're causing too much change too quickly.

Snap!

Activities like burning fossil fuels, such as gas in cars, release greenhouse gases, which keep more heat on the planet's surface and in the atmosphere.

But what can we do about it? Everyone has cars.

There is so much we can do!

Even you and I as individuals can make an impact.

Mostly it requires changing your thinking. Which will be easy for someone your age.

The easiest place to start is the Three Rs.

Oh, I know *this!* Reduce, reuse, recycle.

We *reduce* first because it's most important. The best way to save resources is to cut how much we use to begin with.

When you decide to buy something, make sure to get the most out of it. That's *reuse.*

Look for used items—bikes, clothing—and repair them. Avoid single-use items such as cotton swabs and plastic straws.

People are making *zero-waste* replacements for single-use items all the time!

Like your glass straw.

Tink!

Finally, after you've used something up, *recycle* it. So make sure that what you buy is recyclable.

A soda bottle is a more sustainable choice than a polystyrene cup because plastic is recyclable. Polystyrene takes millions of years to break down. Glass bottles are even better because they are more widely recycled.

Better to recycle the material than throw it in the dump where it can lay for millennia.

What goes in there? Is that also recycling?

Yeah, it's a compost bin. That's where we recycle food scraps!

Gross.

It's actually incredibly useful.

We toss in anything compostable, meaning it can be eaten by bacteria and worms without leaving metals or toxins behind. We toss in our vegetable trimmings. In return, we get rich soil to grow more vegetables.

Oh, right! The soil cycle.

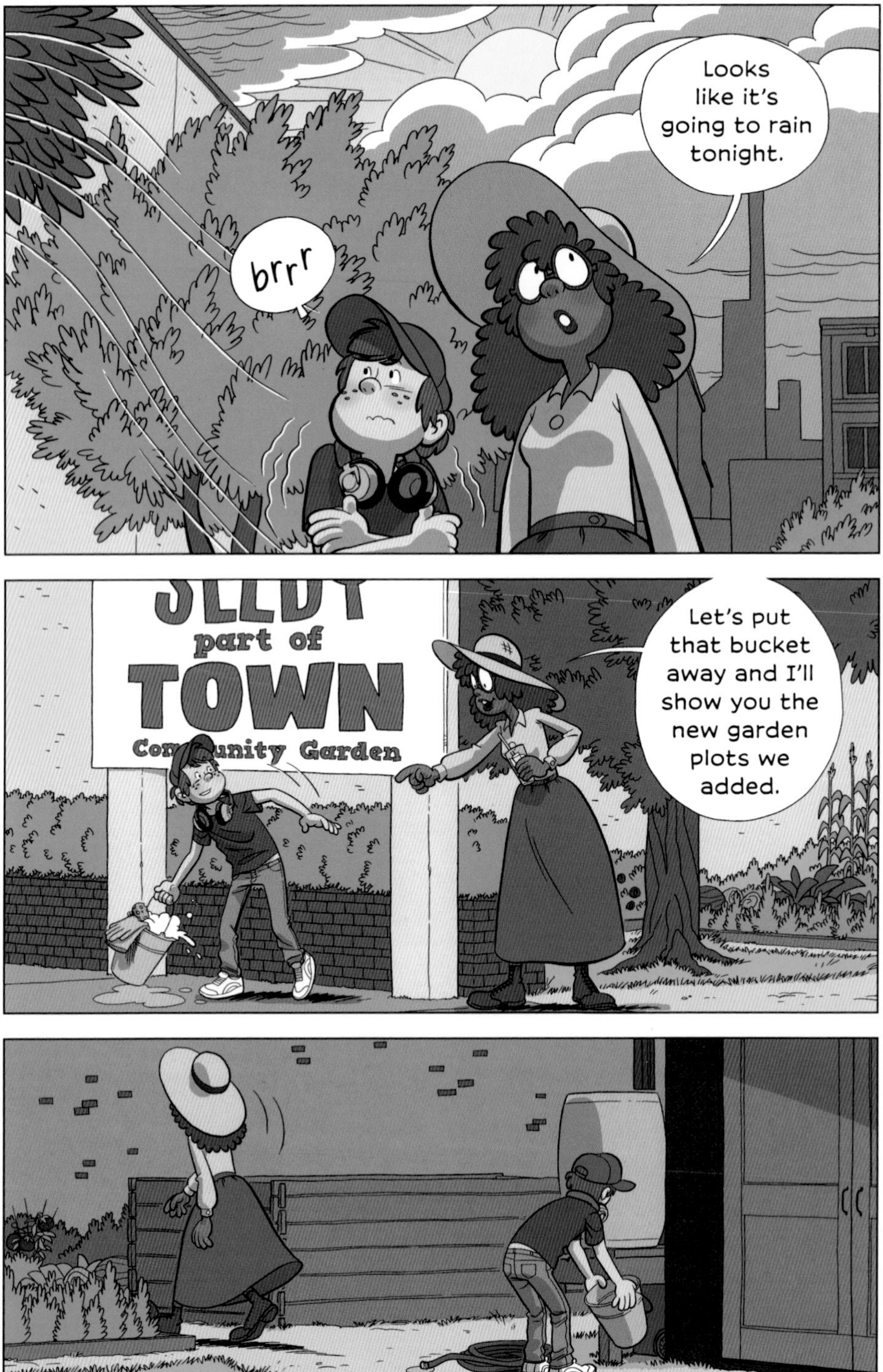
Looks like it's going to rain tonight.
brrr
part of
TOWN
Garden
Let's put that bucket away and I'll show you the new garden plots we added.

The new plots need some *rain barrels* to collect rain for later use.

Why collect rain? I saw someone getting water from the hose over there earlier.

Because of the first R...

Oh, right. Reduce!

Indeed. We have a rain barrel under the shed's gutter downspout to collect roof runoff. That hose is connected to the rain barrel.

Back here, we have open rain barrels that simply catch the rain as it falls. Hi, Esau.

Hi, guys.

Making a Rain Barrel

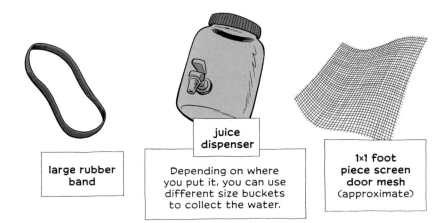

large rubber band

juice dispenser

Depending on where you put it, you can use different size buckets to collect the water.

1×1 foot piece screen door mesh (approximate)

I just have a balcony at home.

Use a juice dispenser! It has a spigot at the bottom so you can pour the water into a cup or watering can to use it.

Why don't you take this one home? You can set it up on your balcony.

I brought it here to see if someone wanted it.

Thanks, Esau! Isaac, here's what you'll do when you get home.

Cover the top of your dispenser with fine mesh—especially if your area has mosquitoes*—and secure it with a rubber band.

* Mosquitoes lay their larva in standing water.

Place your rain barrel where it will get rained on.

As it fills, use the spigot on your juice dispenser to pour water into your watering can. You can water your indoor plants!

If you don't have a juice dispenser, use a washed five-gallon bucket with mesh covering the top. To use the water, take the mesh off, and dunk in a cup or watering can. Then re-cover.

If your house has a rain spout, place a fifty-gallon barrel under the spout and wait for it to fill.

You might need an adult's help to shorten the spout for the barrel to fit under it. We cut this one to end right above the rain barrel filter.

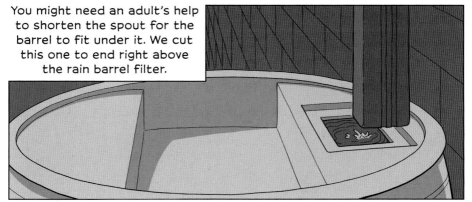

Some large barrels have a spigot at the bottom. You can use a no-flow or zero-flow soaker hose, compensating for the low-pressure, to water your garden or to wash your car.

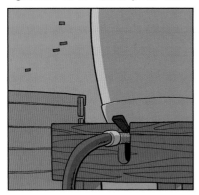

You'll need to check the specs on your rain barrel with an adult to make sure the hose is compatible.

Wow, this is great. Thanks, Esau.

No problem. I'm glad that old juice urn is still useful to someone.

Well, we've done enough today. See you tomorrow, kiddo!

Cool, I'll go set this up now!

Day 2

Good afternoon, Isaac. You have a good day at school?

It was raining, so we had to eat lunch inside.

And now it's hot and muggy!

The sun warms up the ground, evaporating water into the *terror* that is a *muggy day.*

Ugh. It's too hot.

Different surfaces warm and cool at different rates. Concrete holds heat better than soil but also loses it slower. That's why it stays so hot here in the city.

At the farm where I live, the summers cool down in the evening and we get a reprieve.

Gah, I'm coming to your house later for some of that lemonade.

But the ocean covers 70 percent of the planet. It takes that water a long time to cool down.

So, since most of the world is covered in water, the temperature of the whole planet is pretty stable, right?

Yes, but the planet is heating up, which means so are the oceans.

Is that why all our ice is melting, like the polar caps and glaciers?

Water absorbs heat, but ice reflects it. With less ice to reflect heat, the more water there is to absorb it.

And more heat means the ice melts even faster!

And more melted water gets into the oceans. Because the ice caps and glaciers are fresh water, the ocean becomes less salty. If the ocean changes too quickly, the creatures won't be able to adapt.

Whoa. That's, like, so many fish.

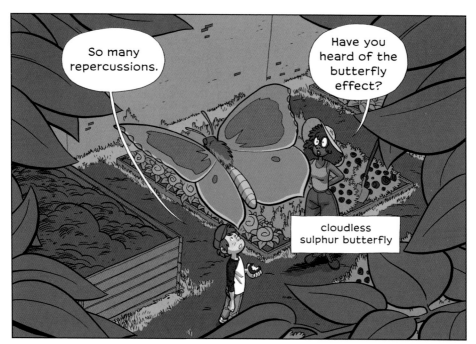

So many repercussions.

Have you heard of the butterfly effect?

cloudless sulphur butterfly

Uh, my teacher said... a butterfly flaps its wings and that tiny action leads to a huge storm. But that's not real, right?

The flap of a butterfly wing can't cause a storm, but little changes can build up in ways we can't predict.

Do you want to see your handiwork? Those rain barrels are filling!

I forgot to check mine. It's probably filling, too.

Whoops!

WHOOOAAAH!

Whoa, there! Nice save.

clap!
clap!
clap!

Aw, man! Not my new sneakers!

Well, you couldn't get nicer mud on your shoes.

What do you mean by that?!

Remember the soil cycle? Healthy soil is full of living organisms. The soil here is as happy and healthy as can be.

ick

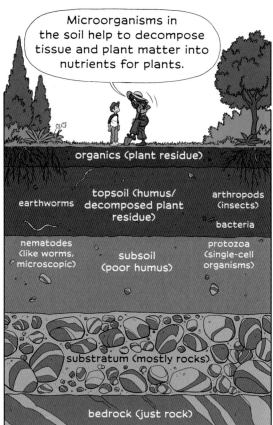

Microorganisms in the soil help to decompose tissue and plant matter into nutrients for plants.

organics (plant residue)

earthworms

topsoil (humus/ decomposed plant residue)

arthropods (insects)

bacteria

nematodes (like worms, microscopic)

subsoil (poor humus)

protozoa (single-cell organisms)

substratum (mostly rocks)

bedrock (just rock)

Worms and bacteria churn out rich topsoil, aka *humus,* cakey and dark brown.

Poop again?

Yes, but worm poop is called *castings* and makes the soil incredibly rich, full of nutrients.

Plants use and deposit specific nutrients. You can take advantage of this by planting crops that benefit each other—companion planting.

Oh! Let's see Rowan. She has a great example.

Hi, Rowan. I wanted to show Isaac your Three Sisters.

How many sisters?!

Ha-ha! I do have one but the Three Sisters are a planting technique.

Way before European settlement, the Three Sisters were the main crops of various indigenous North American communities. It's still commonly used by home gardeners.

Like a good older sister, maize, aka corn, provides support, a structure for the climbing bean vine.

Looks good, Rowan.

Beans, the giving sister, add nitrogen to the soil, which some farmers do using fertilizers. Beans also wind around and hold all three together.

The protecting sister, winter squash, spreads along the ground to block sunlight, a living *mulch.*

It helps eliminate weeds, keep the soil moist, and deter predators with its prickly hairs.

30

Like companion planting, plants grow symbiotically with mushrooms, depending on and supporting each other.

Under the soil, where it's hard to see, there's mycorrhizal fungus. You'll see little mushrooms popping out of the ground.

Mushrooms are cool! Did you know the largest living organism in the world is a single fungus, the Humongous Fungus, *Armillaria ostoyae.*

It covers 2,385 acres in Malheur National Forest in Oregon!

You're a mushroom expert?!

We went to Oregon a couple summers ago, and Dad read us all sorts of facts about the area. I was hoping for a forest of giant mushrooms.

There's no fungus among us!

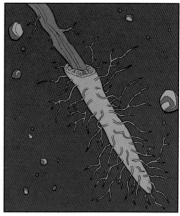

Mycorrhizae are the invisible guardians in healthy soil. They also live in gardens like ours. That's why we don't till our soil—to keep the mycorrhizae intact.

They look like roots but are actually tiny fungal filaments. They wrap around the plant's roots, helping the plants extract water and nutrients. The mycorrhizae become like an extension of the roots, sharing nutrients.

They also protect roots by attacking toxins and disease with enzymes.

Ugh, you know what's attacking?

All these worms!

Where did they come from? Is it an invasion?

Well...

You could consider it an invasion—the good kind. All these worms mean we have really healthy soil. They are drawn to our soil and make it more nutritious through their castings.

Did you notice all the robins we have right now, too?

After a good rain, it doesn't take an early bird to get a worm!

The worms have to come out of the waterlogged soil to breathe.

HUFF! GASP!

Poor guys are just trying to catch a breath!

If you're feeling bad for the worms, why don't we build a worm farm?

A *worm farm* is a type of composting. In regular composting, already-present bacteria use water and oxygen to break down plant material into compost for the garden.

Nature's recycling.

Yeah! Grab that apple you had earlier and toss it in!

In a compost bin, we are making a condensed version of the forest floor...

Making that humus we talked about.

Bacteria, fungi, mites, worms, millipedes, and pill bugs break down the food.

BUILDING A WORM FARM

cool, dry place for farm

plain vegetable and fruit scraps

short red worms (*Eisenia fetida*) or **native worms**

2 plastic, opaque containers (same) about 2x1.5x1.5 feet (smaller is fine, like a garbage can)

large nail and hammer, or a **1/8-inch drill**

soil, either dug up or purchased—with help from an adult

4 empty cans/jars, same height, washed (be careful of sharp edges on cans)

newspaper or corrugated cardboard, in small pieces Black-and-white newsprint is best because it has the least ink. Avoid glossy paper.

1 lid (optional, but recommended) to contain the scent, prevent things from falling in, and ensure a dark environment

We're going to reuse these plastic bins I found behind the grocery store.

What a find...

One already has a lid, and we'll reuse it instead of throwing it away.

If we couldn't find bins to reuse, we could buy new ones made from 100% recycled plastic.

With an adult, use a hammer and nail to poke holes in the bottom and sides of one bin for air and drainage. Make the holes in a grid 6 inches apart on the bottom and 10 inches on the sides. If you have one, put 6 holes evenly spaced in the lid. Make these holes on the grass or a scrap of wood.

Or an adult can help you use a drill with a 1/8-inch bit to drill the holes.

Place your four empty cans evenly in the other bin, open sides down. Put the holey container inside, on top of the cans for drainage.

Fill the top bin in layers: 4 inches of shredded paper, thin layer of vegetable scraps, 2 inches of soil. Repeat for 2/3 of the container, ending with soil. Altogether, these layers make up the bedding for the worms.

Aw.

z

Water the bedding until it's damp but not sopping.

Worms can't breathe in soil that's too wet.

Add worms! You can get short red ones at your local garden center or online. They are voracious eaters, making lots of castings. Earthworms look cool but aren't big eaters. Since red wigglers are from Europe, you can ask your garden center or extension office (soil and wildlife department) which local worms are the biggest eaters.

If you have a lid, place it on top. Keep your worm farm in a dark place, not too warm and not too cool. You need access so you can easily feed them.

I'll put them under the kitchen sink.

Every few months, pour out the liquid from the lower bin. Thin it with 10 parts water as fertilizer.

Now you can feed them! They want fruit (no citrus), vegetables, coffee grounds, bread, or leaves from the yard.

Do not feed them meat, dairy, citrus, spices, salt, oil, fat, or pet feces. Worms don't like it and it will rot. Rot deprives the worms of oxygen so they can't breathe.

To feed them, about once a week dig a hole in the bedding and place the scraps in it. (They can eat half their weight per day.) Cover the hole with the dirt. If the food rots, just pick it out and feed them less.

Put the scraps in a new spot each time so the castings get spread around. Cover the top with newspaper if it gets smelly or if you don't have a lid.

Scoot scoot, little guys. It's din-din time!

Change the bedding twice a year: dump it out on a tarp, pick out the worms—removing any dead ones—and remake the bedding as before with the same worms. The soil will be rich to plant in, so add it to your garden or replant potted plants.

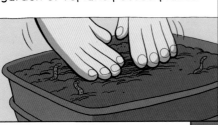

Wow, these are going to be the most useful pets I've ever had!

Just be careful not to play with the worms. They have a lot of work to do!

Day 3

They took them! My most prized possession!

Calm down, Ajeet. It happens. You'll grow more.

But I look forward to these carrots all year.

boo hoo

What happened?

Ajeet's carrots have been gobbled up.

Was it... **rabbits?!** I didn't know rabbits lived in the city.

Probably not. It was more likely weevils or groundhogs. Rabbits eat leafy greens.

But their camouflage is very good. Look, there's one now.

Don't tell Ajeet.

What can we do about them?

Losing your plants is disappointing, but animals are part of the ecosystem. If there's other food for them, you can keep rabbits out by installing fences. Also, a weeded garden leaves no hiding places. If I find rabbits out during the day, I just...

...shoo, shoo.

There's another rabbit.

And another one!

Another what?

Nothing....

Another...

...dandelion.

Why are there so many rabbits?

That is a more complicated question than you think.

They might have been here when the city was built, or expanded and adapted to the new circumstances.

Or their home outside the city became too inhospitable from farming or habitat destruction.

Lots of wildlife has joined us in urban areas: pigeons, rats, mice, cockroaches, squirrels, and even foxes and deer.

They've adapted to our living situations. Many would rather not live among humans, but with the cities growing, the options become fewer.

Some animals can't adapt like these rabbits have. Like orangutans.

They live in rain forests on the islands of Borneo and Sumatra, in Southeast Asia.

But the forests are being destroyed for palm oil plantations. Orangutans aren't as adaptable as rabbits, so their populations are in decline.

Is there anything we can do?

For orangutans, we can avoid products with *destructive* palm oil, which is in many items, such as bread, cereal, ice cream, soap. Read labels for responsible palm oil.*

But on a larger scale, we can make choices in our urban planning and the material we use to accommodate wildlife.

CERTIFIED SUSTAINABLE PALM OIL
· RSPO ·

SEEDY part of TOWN

* Palm oil is in half the items you see in a grocery store, mostly prepared foods. But look for the RSPO (Roundtable on Sustainable Palm Oil) logo. There's also an app from Cheyenne Mountain Zoo called Sustainable Palm Oil Shopping.

We can preserve locations that are home to endangered populations. For example, we protect wetlands with fences, or put restrictions on how they can be used.

People aren't allowed to build on these preservations.

There's a wetland by my aunt's house where we visit the ducks.

We can also include wildlife bridges on roads. These provide safe passage for animals to cross.

If we adopt a road, we can clean it up, but we can also try to make it safer for the animals by working with the city—for example, adding those signs and wildlife bridges, especially on faster roads like highways and freeways.

I saw a family of deer using the cross-walk the other day.

Yeah, animals can be very smart.

My school once held a "green walk" where we all got gloves and garbage bags.

We had to walk around in groups picking up trash in our school's neighborhood.

Green walks are a wonderful way to make our neighborhoods less dangerous for the animals. Our garbage can hurt them!

The grossest thing I picked up was a pile of shrimp tails.

But someone else found a full dirty diaper!

I really did notice a difference in how nice the neighborhood looked when we were done.

That's how I feel when I do the dishes at my house.

What other animals have you seen around here? Have you ever seen a fox?

I haven't seen any, but they are nocturnal so we are unlikely to see them.

I saw an opossum on the sidewalk once. I wanted to get a better look, but he smelled terrible.

Someone probably scared him. Their coping mechanism is to feign death, including the smell. But other than that, they are clean and helpful, eating a lot of ticks.

I think I'd prefer that to the raccoon who raids our dumpster. Those teeth. *Terrifying.*

You have quite the eye for local wildlife.

They are fascinating.

There was a pigeon in my neighborhood who had only one eye!

I tried to feed it a peanut, because that's what I feed the crow with the bad leg. But the poor pigeon couldn't open the shell.

So I looked up what to feed him and ended up giving him some cracked corn instead.

It's good you did some research before feeding the wildlife—sometimes it can be dangerous for you or harmful to them!

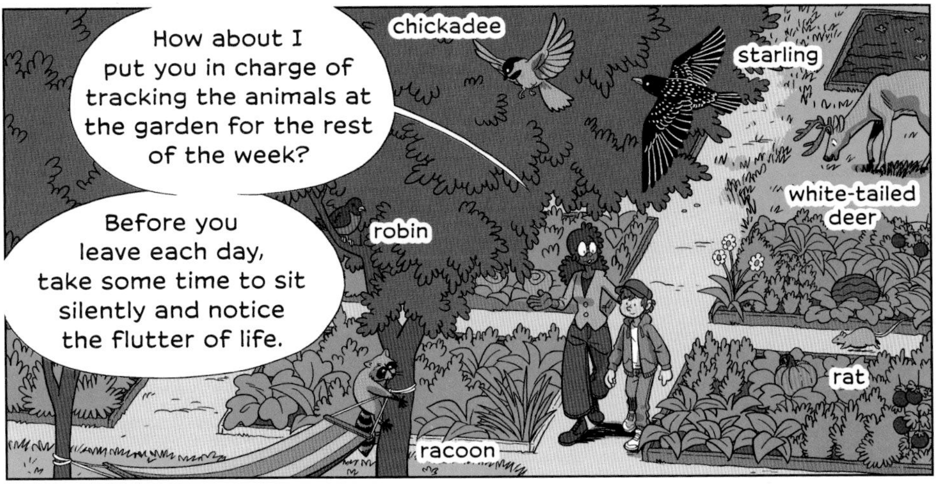
How about I put you in charge of tracking the animals at the garden for the rest of the week?
Before you leave each day, take some time to sit silently and notice the flutter of life.
chickadee
starling
white-tailed deer
robin
rat
racoon

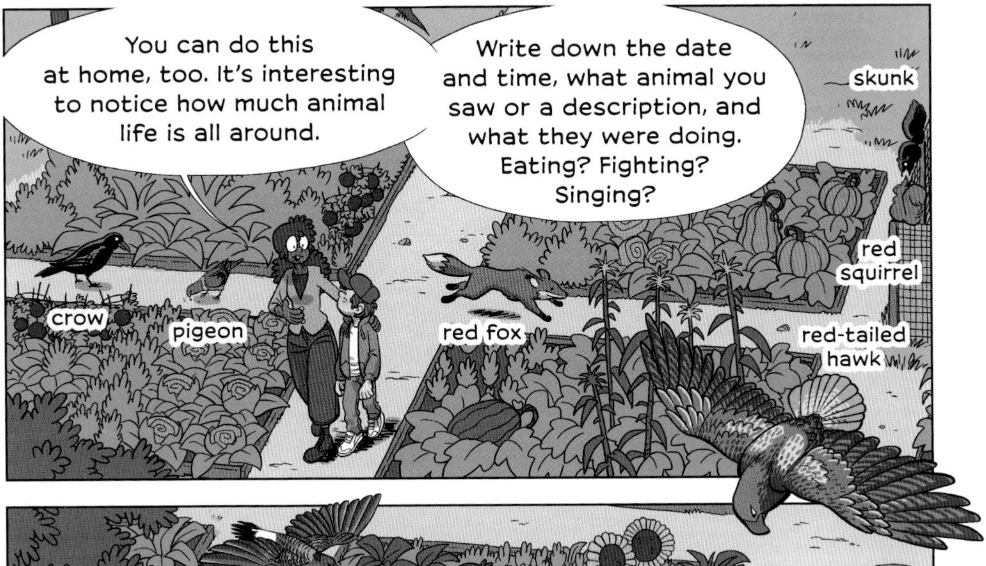
You can do this at home, too. It's interesting to notice how much animal life is all around.
Write down the date and time, what animal you saw or a description, and what they were doing. Eating? Fighting? Singing?
skunk
red squirrel
crow
pigeon
red fox
red-tailed hawk

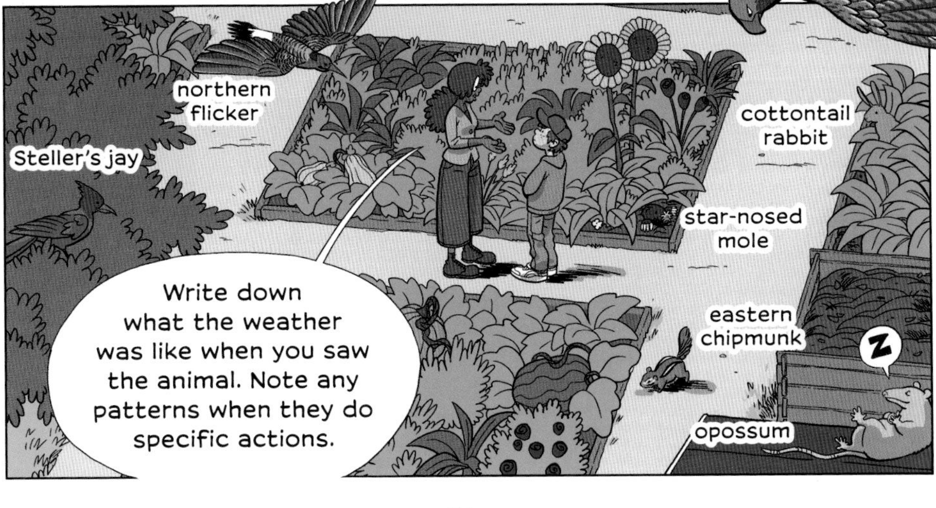
northern flicker
Steller's jay
cottontail rabbit
star-nosed mole
Write down what the weather was like when you saw the animal. Note any patterns when they do specific actions.
eastern chipmunk
Z
opossum

If you move slowly and don't startle them, you can take a picture with your phone.

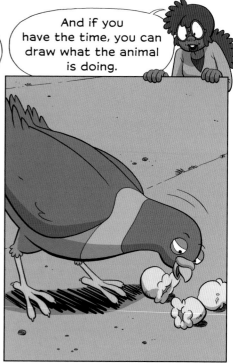

And if you have the time, you can draw what the animal is doing.

With time and care, you can start to recognize specific individuals.

Like that pigeon, Sir Squints-a-Lot!

And don't forget the insects! Insects that don't fly can't get away as fast, so you can use a magnifying glass.

I'll go buy a notebook to write all the animals in!

But, Isaac, what about the Three Rs? We can make you one from recycled materials instead.

Binding a Recycled Notebook

5 or so sheets of copy paper (one side can be used—check the recycling bin at your school or library)

cereal box or heavy paper stock

large needle

scissors

cutting board

spoon (optional)

thumbtack

embroidery floss

paper cutter (optional)

Cut the cardboard to the same size as your copy paper. This will be your cover. You can use scissors, but a paper cutter gives a more uniform cut.

Neatly stack your copy paper so all the edges line up. Fold the stack in half. For a nice, crisp fold, use the bottom of a spoon to crease the paper.

For your cover, decide if you want the blank side out or the printed side out. Then fold it in half like the copy paper.

Unfold the paper and cardboard. Stack the cardboard under the paper so the folds nestle together.

Put a cutting board under your paper. With your thumbtack, poke three holes straight through the fold—in the middle and about an inch from the edge on each end.

Time to sew! Thread your needle: put your floss through the eye of your needle and pull about one third through. Do not tie a knot at the end.

You can use yarn or string, but you might need a larger needle.

Go in the middle from the outside, leaving a few inches of tail.

Go out the top hole...

...in the bottom hole...

...and out the middle hole again.

Tie a knot with the two tails around the center thread.

You can draw or write on the cover, or glue on cutouts. Find upcycled decorations instead of stickers and glitter.

Now you can draw and write in your book. If there is already something printed on the page, you can skip it.

What, waste a page? I like to draw over the stuff that's already there.

I can draw the rabbits we saw today!

By making a recycled notebook, I reduced the amount of new paper I'm using! That's two for three.

You sure did! About four billion trees are cut down across the globe every year to create paper, so it's a great place to practice reducing.

With recycled paper, triple word score, that's all three!

For trees to grow to full size, it can take decades, even hundreds of years, depending on the species.

Cutting them down is wasteful, so we should get as much use out of them as we can.

There are other options, like post-consumer waste, or recycled paper. If it's 100 percent recycled, no trees were cut down. Even 50 percent or 10 percent is a reduction.

We don't need to make paper out of trees. These are all fast-growing, maturing after only a year.

kenaf

cotton

hemp

bamboo

Bamboo can grow in depleted soil, and some species can grow more than one foot in a day.

That's a lot of pulp.

Phew.

This is tough work.

Another easy way to reduce is lowering power consumption. That's why we're using clippers instead of a powered hedge trimmer. There's also lots of ways to get energy for our homes.

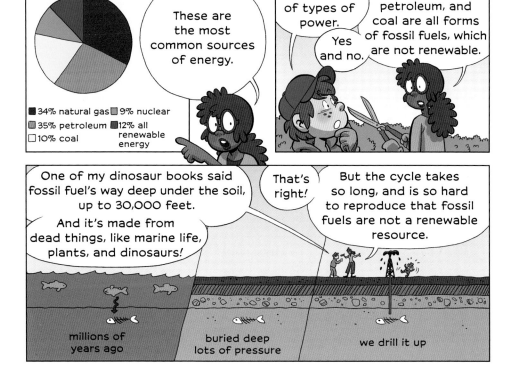

These are the most common sources of energy.

- ■ 34% natural gas
- ▨ 35% petroleum
- ☐ 10% coal
- ☐ 9% nuclear
- ▩ 12% all renewable energy

That's a lot of types of power.

Yes and no.

Natural gas, petroleum, and coal are all forms of fossil fuels, which are not renewable.

One of my dinosaur books said fossil fuel's way deep under the soil, up to 30,000 feet.

And it's made from dead things, like marine life, plants, and dinosaurs!

That's right!

But the cycle takes so long, and is so hard to reproduce that fossil fuels are not a renewable resource.

millions of years ago

buried deep lots of pressure

we drill it up

Nuclear is those huge reactors, right? Dad said they're cleaner because they don't burn coal or gas. But they do make radioactive waste. Right?

Partly. Nuclear reactors generate steam by heating water with uranium, usually. The steam turns huge turbines that generate electricity. But uranium mines do pollute. Nuclear waste is nearly impossible to dispose of safely.

So what renewable energy sources are there?

All sorts!

We can actually get power from solar panels. The panels collect light from the sun and convert it into electricity. This works great in sunny locations.

Solar panels provide energy with no outright pollution.

What do you mean "no outright pollution"?

The panels don't pollute, but creating them does.

Argh! We just can't win.

They are made with rare Earth metals—seventeen unique elements on the periodic table. Mining for these metals puts out a lot of pollution and is really destructive to the local environment.

Right. And we can't make more of them.

Isn't there's water power? Like the Hoover Dam? We went there on vacation once. It was the world's tallest dam until 2013.

Hydropower is a great example of alternative energy. We get clean energy with little to no pollution.

But there can be downsides. Some of the dams are in the way of migrating fish.

Salmon must return to their birthplace to lay eggs. If they can't, their species could die out.

We can work around it with fish ladders...

And fish tubes!

...which are like water stairs fish can jump up to get past the dam. We can also be aware of spawning routes when building dams.

In general, we should be aware of animals in the area when expanding cities in urban planning!

We should have planned around those rabbits.

If there's so many other options, why do we use fossil fuels?

Fossil fuels are easy, cheap, and powerful. They're a miracle material, and we use them every day to fuel our cars and airplanes, to heat our homes, and to generate electricity.

Fossil fuels come from many different sources, like converting crude oil to gasoline, harvesting natural gas from under ground, and mining coal.

Petroleum, the liquid form of fossil fuel, is very versatile. Through "miracles of modern science," we use it to make clothes (acrylic, polyester, nylon), plastics (grocery bags, soda bottles, console game bodies), and more.

But we're running out of easily accessible fossil fuels after using oil for less than 150 years. Even "easy-access" fuel can cause environmental problems, such as polluting groundwater and oceans.

Oil is far under the surface, so we drill through the Earth's mantle to extract it. To save time and energy, we drill through the thinnest part of the mantle. And it's thinnest under the ocean.

mantle – the solid layer deep under the crust of soil,

And then there are oil spills, right?

Yes, because we're all just human. But when there's an oil spill, like the Gulf of Mexico in 1979, it devastates the wildlife. That was the second worst oil spill in history, pouring 454,000 tons of oil into the gulf for about nine months. In 2018 alone, we had 137 oil spills ranging from 2.1 million gallons to just 30.

African penguin

That poor bird.

Being covered in oil prevents birds from flying and fish from breathing.

Yeah.

Those poor animals.

But, when disaster strikes, people are willing to lend a hand and wash those birds.

They literally use dish soap.

Washing birds sounds more fun and rewarding than washing dishes.

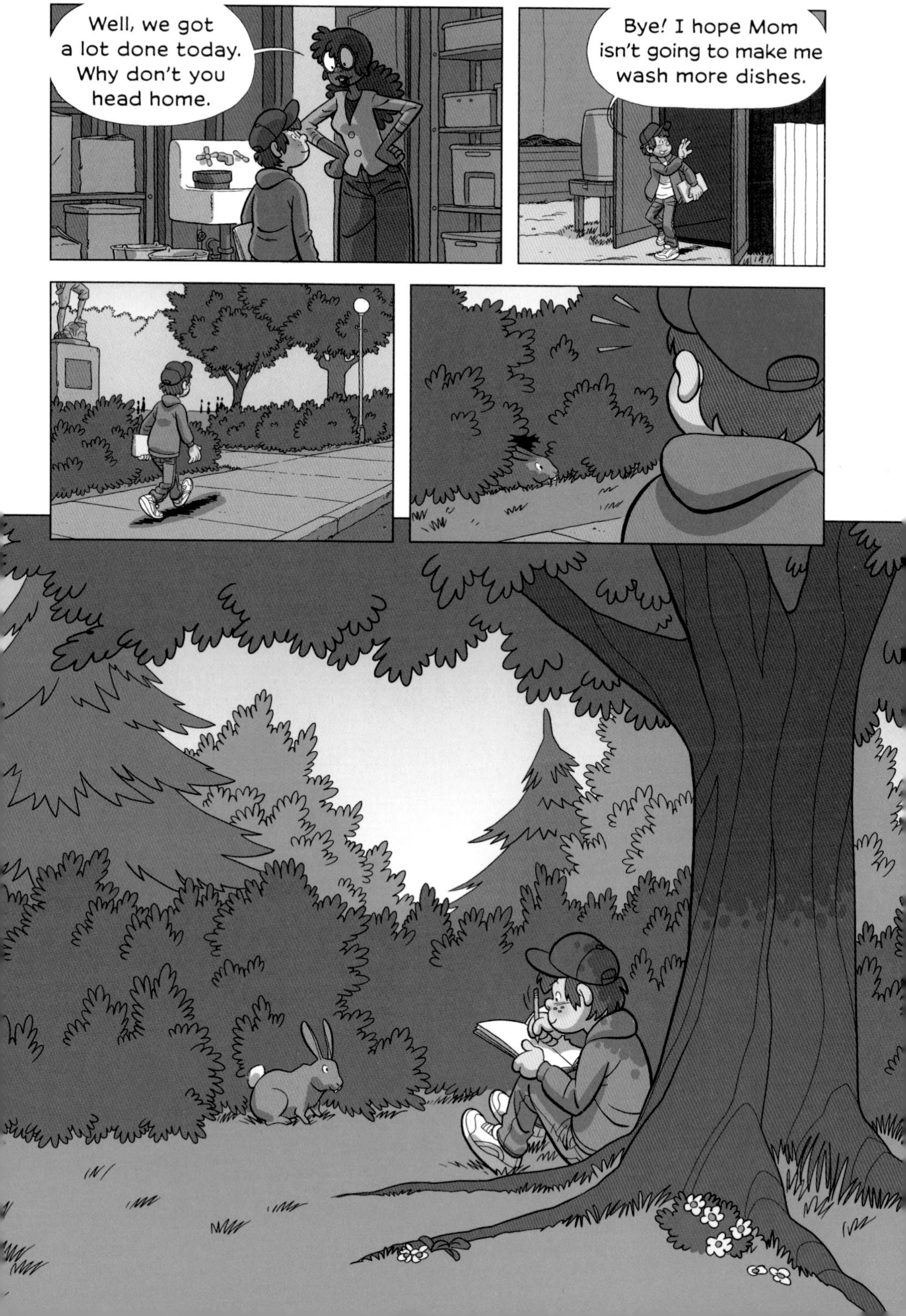
Well, we got a lot done today. Why don't you head home.
Bye! I hope Mom isn't going to make me wash more dishes.

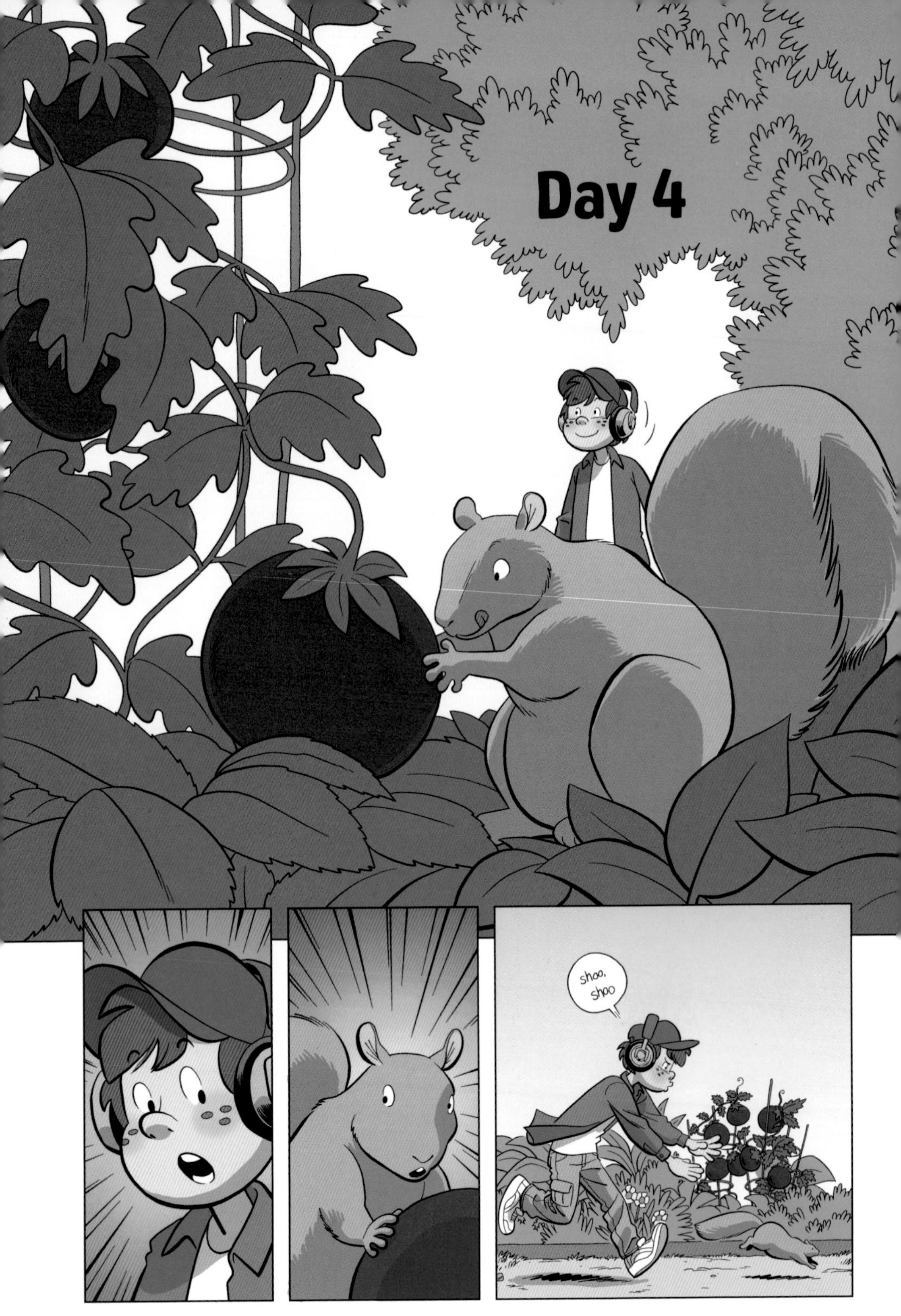
Day 4
shoo,
shoo

Good morning, Isaac. Well spotted and well done! We'll make an urban farmer of you yet.

Isaac, did you just save my tomato from the dratted squirrel? Thank you, young squire!

It was nothing, Nova. I was just surprised that squirrel would eat a tomato right off the vine!

I have to reward you somehow. I think one of these perfectly ripe tomatoes would be appropriate.

Here you go.

I don't know what to say...

Thank you?

While I have you, Aurora, would you mind watering my tomatoes while I'm away on vacation next week?

Of course.

Why don't we use a sprinkler system so everyone's plants get watered even if they can't come out?

Simply one of the Three Rs: Reduce. We don't want to willy-nilly spray water where it isn't needed.

Oh.

Right.

It might feel small, but it's simple changes that can make a big difference...

...like using water only when and where it's needed.

You can easily reduce your use of water and energy through some simple changes. And you can refuse some things, stopping them altogether.

You must drink water every day, but you can limit other uses. Turn off the water when you're washing dishes or brushing your teeth.

I already do that!

Your parents might be able to install a low-flow showerhead.

That's not always an option, but even just cutting one minute from your shower saves four gallons of water or more.

I could cut my showers down to once a week.

...That's not necessary.

But every other day is a simple way to cut your use by 50 percent! And baths should definitely be an occasional treat—they use almost twice the water of a shower.

I could save energy by turning off the lights I'm not using.

You got it!

You can also use LED light bulbs instead of traditional incandescent lights. The LEDs use less power and last longer.

LED

incandescent

When it gets cold...

I can use blankets and sweaters instead of turning on the heat. At least before it gets *too* cold. It gets pretty chilly in this part of the country.

It can sure be hard to remember that in the summer, though.

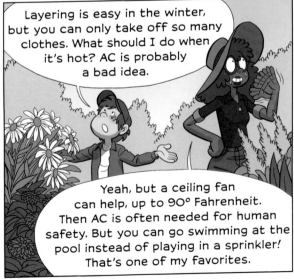

Layering is easy in the winter, but you can only take off so many clothes. What should I do when it's hot? AC is probably a bad idea.

Yeah, but a ceiling fan can help, up to 90° Fahrenheit. Then AC is often needed for human safety. But you can go swimming at the pool instead of playing in a sprinkler! That's one of my favorites.

You can save a lot on energy with your transportation choices, too.

I walk here from school and then walk home.

That's great!

And my buddies and I ride our bikes all summer.

That's helpful on two fronts. Saves your car's gas and your parents' time, which I am sure they appreciate.

And if it's too far to bike or walk, you can carpool or take public transportation! The per-person carbon footprint's much lower because they transport so many people at once.

Electric vehicles create less pollution and, depending on your electricity source, can mostly bypass fossil fuels. They just use a bit of oil for lubrication.

I saw our buses might switch to electric or biodiesel. But what is biodiesel?

It's renewable fuel made from vegetable oils, animal fats, or used restaurant grease, though it can be hard on engines.

Isaac! Oh, Isaac!

I could use your youthful strength over here!

Sure thing.

Please Romaine Calm, our friendly neighborhood garden center, dropped off my new Empire apple tree sapling. Come help me carry it over to the plot.

Pivot!

Pivot!

Alright...

...just a little farther now.

My shirt!

RRRRIIIIP

AAAUGH!

Isaac, are you okay?

Oh, good. It's just a tear.

Just a tear?! Now I have to throw away this shirt!

And I kind of liked it.

You don't need to throw this shirt out.

It's a minor tear. We can sew it up right here.

This is another R for you to remember: repair or reuse.

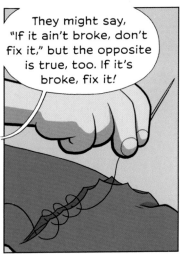

They might say, "If it ain't broke, don't fix it," but the opposite is true, too. If it's broke, fix it!

Ta-da! Good as new. And if you don't like that little seam, you can sew a patch on top.

Yeah, look at my pants!

Wow, not bad.

Thanks for showing me how to fix that, Aurora.

You can reuse and repair many items. Our sewing kit has pre-threaded needles with different colored thread, tiny scissors, and a couple safety pins.

If your item still works, don't replace it. There is no need to have the newest version of everything.

And if you have to get rid of something that still works, resell or donate it! I run a group that trades or gives away items.

I got this hat there!

Oh, like when Esau gave me that juice dispenser so I could make my own rain jug!

When you can, buy used. If you have an item to get rid of and need something else, you might trade items with a friend.

If it's not useable anymore, you can sometimes upcycle it—use it to make a new thing!

With old clothes that are too ruined to donate, you can upcycle them into cleaning rags, pot holders, rugs, or quilts, or even donate them to animal shelters.

And when other things are finally toast—such as bottles, or phones—you can recycle most of them. This is usually a service provided by your local municipality.

To recycle, you usually need to sort out the different types, depending on your local regulations.

electronic equipment

In some places, it's illegal to throw electronics away because they release toxic materials, so you need to check your local recycling regulations.

plastic bags

Try to avoid these—use a tote bag for groceries and small cloth bags for produce. Plastic bags are difficult to recycle, so if you do use them, research your local recycling options. Many grocery stores take them.

It's important to recycle the right way—sort materials as needed and deposit them in the right place. Plastic bags can jam the recycling machinery.

plastic bottles

It's better to avoid these by using reusable water bottles. You can request (or bring) reusable cups when dining out.

aluminum cans and other metals

You can get paid to recycle some metals.

paper

Some of this looks nice enough to reuse as wrapping paper. What we don't reuse, we'll recycle.

glass

Glass is the best option because it's infinitely recyclable. And when it's no longer useful, it turns into sand.

Some cities include yard waste, such as leaves and grass clippings, in the city pickup services. The worms in your worm farm might not be able to eat as much yard waste as you make!

yard waste

So if I pay attention to what I buy, I should be able to reuse things until they're kaput and then recycle them.

But where does the recycling go?

It differs in each region, but in general they go to a recycling center where items are sorted further, such as types of plastic or colors of glass.

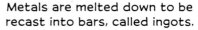

Paper goes to a pulper that mushes it to a slurry, then a de-inker that washes out the ink.

Metals are melted down to be recast into bars, called ingots.

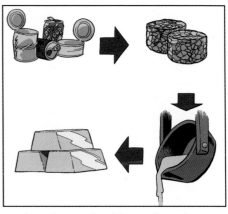

Plastic is separated by type, the number on the bottom, then chopped into bits and melted into a polymer for new products. Unfortunately, it is downcycled—it becomes a lesser version, until it has to be thrown away.

Glass is crushed into tiny pieces called cullet and heated into molten glass to be reused.

Anything they can't accept— stuff they can't recycle or that has food on it—heads to a landfill or incinerator.

What? Even the recycling plants send out garbage?

That's why we need to follow the local recycling rules.

A landfill stores the garbage. It's a container for the items that either don't break down on their own—at least, in a few generations— or break down into toxins due to a lack of oxygen. Landfills have layers of clay and drainpipes to collect the toxic fluid, which is treated at a wastewater treatment plant.

When a landfill is full, it's covered in plastic and then with soil and plants. The garbage breaks down even slower after it's sealed, producing dangerous methane gas. Covering it keeps animals and people away from potential toxins.

Gross!

Or cool? Like the most disgusting time capsule?

Sometimes, instead of burying garbage, we burn it. At an incinerator, garbage is burned in furnaces at 1,800° Fahrenheit!

Youch!

But incinerators aren't great because burning things like plastic releases toxic fumes that are carried by air currents all around the world.

Because safely getting rid of garbage is so difficult, people are constantly thinking of ways to avoid creating it in the first place: reducing packaging, replacing single-use items. For example, there are reusable replacements for cotton swabs, plastic-free shoes, and toothpaste tablets in jars!

Rethinking how you use things is the most difficult part of being more sustainable. But also the most creative.

What else can things be used for? How can we change the things we are used to?

We already reused those old bins to make your worm farm.

Have old paint? Does an artist need it? Or if it is house paint, does a neighbor need it?

Like, I could use some old house paint to paint a mural on the back wall of the garden.

Now that's an interesting idea.

If you come up with a grand idea like a neighborhood swap, get your parents to help you talk with the city council! Adults love kids with *gumption*.

Start thinking outside the box and getting involved!

So what can I do when I need to buy new clothes?

Good question. There's always thrift stores. Or you could look into vintage clothing for fancier gear. Or even swap with friends!

But when you must buy something new, sometimes it boils down to not buying the cheapest thing you can find.

The cost savings come from cheap labor—paying workers low wages, providing poor working conditions—and cheap materials, usually due to less environmental protection. Cheap fabrics like polyester require lots of energy to make and use toxic chemicals.

But what about this shirt? It was $10 I saved from my allowance. I love this shirt!

Good thing we fixed it instead of tossing it. If you have it already, make as much use of it as you can.

And next time, think about how your clothing is made. Choose natural fibers like organic cotton and wool, or peace silk.

flax

hemp

bamboo

alpaca

Peace silk? It's not the seventies!

Ah, a glorious time, ha-ha. Peace silk means it doesn't kill the silkworm to get the silk.

And think about whether you need that heavily dyed shirt. Synthetic dyes contain harmful chemicals and use a lot of water.

White isn't much better because it's bleached with chlorine.

So, like undyed natural cotton? That's better?

Yeah. There are also natural fabric dyes made from organic matter, but that doesn't mean just brown. Indigo plants make blue dye. Some people use cochineal—dried insects—for red dye.

And take a look at that label. If it was made in the US or Canada, the clothes didn't have to travel as far.

MADE IN CHINA

Wait, are you still delicately holding that tomato? Here, take half of this cucumber. You can make a salad for your family.

Let's make reusable food wrappers to put them in. That's a great way we can know where our item was made and with what materials—DIY*!

* Do It Yourself

fabric, 9×9-inch squares
(wash before using)

Organic cotton, such as sheets, is best. But high thread count is most important—you shouldn't be able to see through the cloth.

scissors

Or pinking shears, which cut a zigzag edge to prevent the fabric from unraveling.

food grater

for the beeswax brick

beeswax

You can get this online in bricks and grate it, or in preformed beads. Try to get organic beeswax, though. Cosmetic grade has more impurities than food grade, but is typically fine if you aren't allergic to bees.

Creating Reusable Food Wrappers

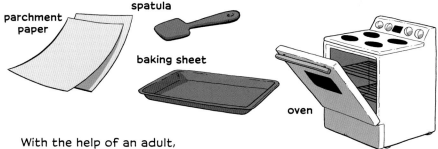

parchment paper

spatula

baking sheet

oven

With the help of an adult, preheat the oven to low, around 200° Fahrenheit. You need the lowest setting because wax fumes can catch on fire at higher temperatures.

This is one use we have for our oven. Also, drying herbs and hosting potlucks.

Cut your cloth into squares, about 9x9 inches. You don't have to be precise.

Put the parchment paper over your baking sheet. It should be about the same size as the baking sheet, larger than your fabric.

Place a piece of the fabric on the parchment paper.

Grate the beeswax onto the fabric (or pour the beads over). You'll want the fabric covered. Be generous. Smooth it out so the fabric is covered like perfect nachos.

Put the sheet in the oven for 10–15 minutes until all the wax is melted.

Remove the sheet and use a spatula to smooth the liquid wax over the fabric so it is entirely saturated. Get all the way to the edge, which keeps the fabric from coming apart. It's okay if the wax gets on the paper.

Leave the food wrapper flat on parchment paper to dry for about an hour. When it is cool to the touch and no longer sticky, it's ready for wrapping. You can keep the parchment paper to use for your next food wrappers, too.

CAUTION: Be very careful with the wax. It will be hot enough to burn you! It will be like water right after it comes out of the oven, but it cools and dries quickly.

An hour later

So I use this instead of plastic wrap?

Correct! And when you're done each time, handwash it in cold water with alcohol-free soap. Cold water makes it stiff so you can wash it pretty easily.

And if it starts getting floppy, it's running out of wax, so I can just melt more on, right?

Correct again! You are really getting the hang of this.

Let's wrap those veggies before you head home.

Oh, the heat of my hands melts the wax just enough that it sticks to itself. *Cool!*

Or *hot* as the case may be.

GROAN!

Day 5

♪

Hi, Aurora.

WHOA!

What happened?

A bee tried to fly into my mouth!

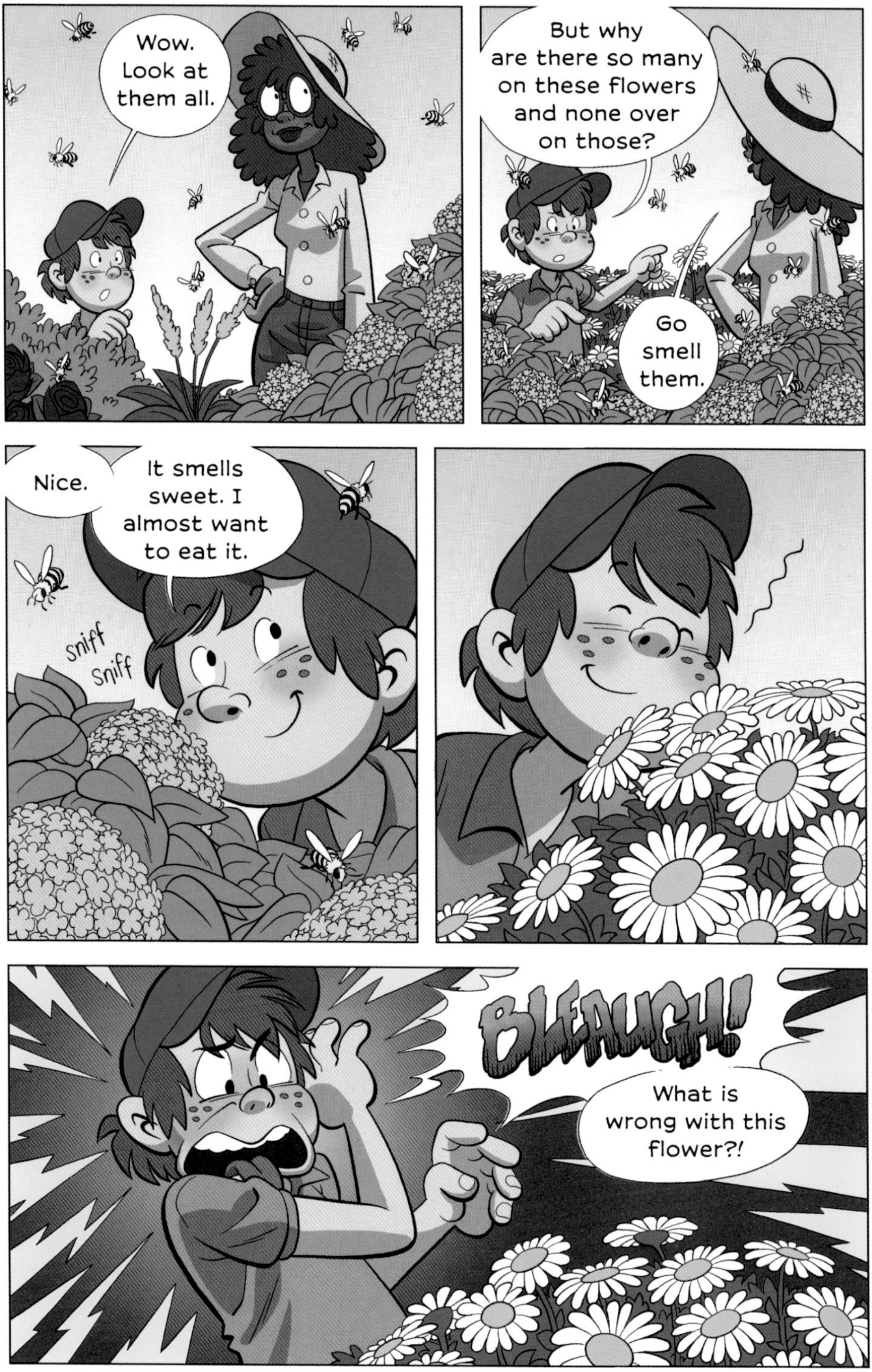
Wow. Look at them all.
But why are there so many on these flowers and none over on those?
Go smell them.
Nice.
It smells sweet. I almost want to eat it.
sniff sniff
BLEAUGH!
What is wrong with this flower?!

Flowers need *pollinators* to move pollen from one flower to another to produce fruit. Good-smelling flowers like this lilac typically attract bees.

And bad-smelling flowers like the Shasta daisy attract flies.

Flies? Gross. I thought they ate poop and garbage.

Well, that, too. But stinky smells indicates moist rot, perfect for flies' eggs and larvae. Different plants *coevolved* with different pollinators—meaning they depend on each other. Bees, flies, butterflies, birds, and wind can be pollinators. Even mammals and reptiles!

Darwin's moth

Darwin's orchid

Look at this milkweed. We planted it for the monarch butterflies.

Plants are important to our lives because not only are some food, but they make oxygen for us to breathe and clean the air.

light

oxygen

CO_2

sugar

water

minerals

So we need to keep pollinators healthy, too, since neither can survive without the other. And we can't survive without either of them.

One way to make plants and their pollinators happy and safe is through permaculture.

clematis

Permaculture is a conscious decision to create a diverse, stable, and resilient environment. Beyond being sustainable, it's regenerative.

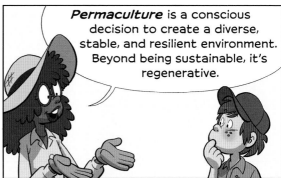

When designing a permaculture garden, aim for a closed loop system, using as little outside input as possible.

Like the Three Sisters?

Is that permaculture?

Yeah, good memory.

And if your city allows it, you can keep chickens or ducks as pets and let them graze in your garden—they will eat pest insects and their poop will fertilize the soil.

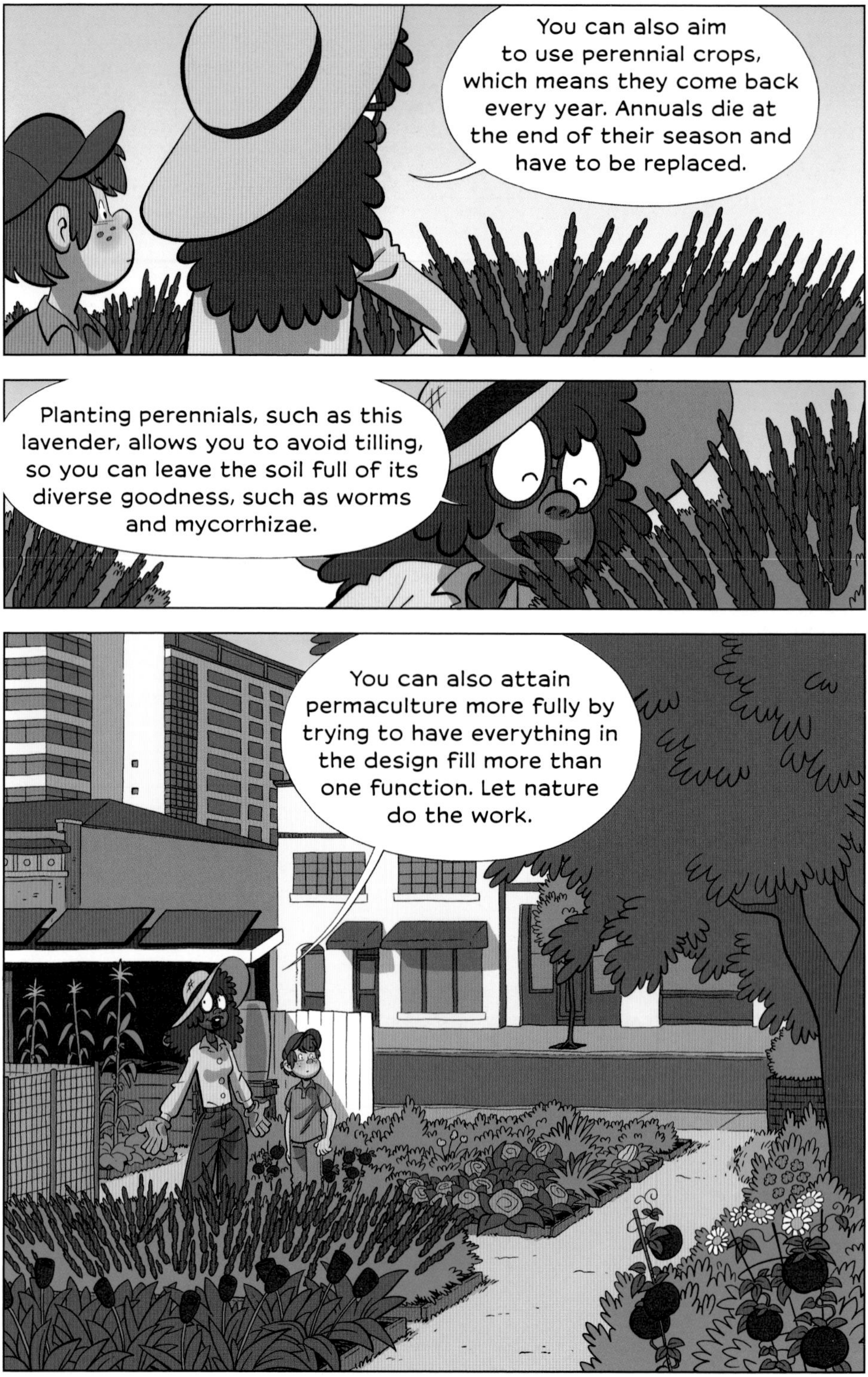
You can also aim to use perennial crops, which means they come back every year. Annuals die at the end of their season and have to be replaced.
Planting perennials, such as this lavender, allows you to avoid tilling, so you can leave the soil full of its diverse goodness, such as worms and mycorrhizae.
You can also attain permaculture more fully by trying to have everything in the design fill more than one function. Let nature do the work.

For example, instead of building a fence, you could plant a hedge. This will provide the privacy and protection of a fence, but also acts as a windbreak by creating a buffer from wind that won't blow over.

If you need something more solid to keep animals and people out, you can paint a fence white to direct extra heat and light to nearby plants.

Or your fence can be a trellis for a vine to grow on. This trellis would also be a windbreak, and painting it white would make a warm reflective surface. If you use it to grow grapes or other fruiting vines, it will also provide food.

If you stick to native plants, you're working toward regeneration by aiding local pollinators.

Native plants and animals are the ones that evolved in the area, right?

Yes. But over human history, we have brought all variety of organisms—birds, insects, plants, animals—to new locations as we travel.

Some of them become invasive species, so successful, and growing in such abundance, that they harm the native ecosystem and throw everything out of whack.

Dad says starlings are an invasive species. But they seem harmless to me.

The problem is they're aggressive and territorial. They kick other birds out of their nests, consume massive amounts of food, and transmit disease.

You know, starlings are European, but Eugene Schieffelin brought sixty starlings to Central Park in New York in the winter of 1890. He wanted to bring every bird in Shakespeare's plays to the US.

And now they cover North America!

The Himalayan blackberry, an invasive species, was introduced to the US in 1885 for its fruit.

They were right. Blackberries are tasty!

But there is a native species of blackberry in the Pacific Northwest. It has smaller fruit and produces less of it.

Pacific blackberry

Himalayan blackberry

The Himalayan blackberry has slipped in well with local pollinators. The plants grow so large, so quickly, that they provide more food for the native bees than the native blackberries can.

Now the Himalayan blackberry is out of control, crowding out the native plants. It's hard to get rid of and will grow over whole buildings.

The Himalayan blackberry is mostly on the West Coast right now, but it is also in patches throughout the Midwest and East Coast. So it's coming for everyone.

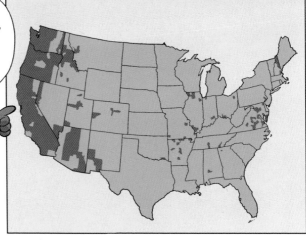

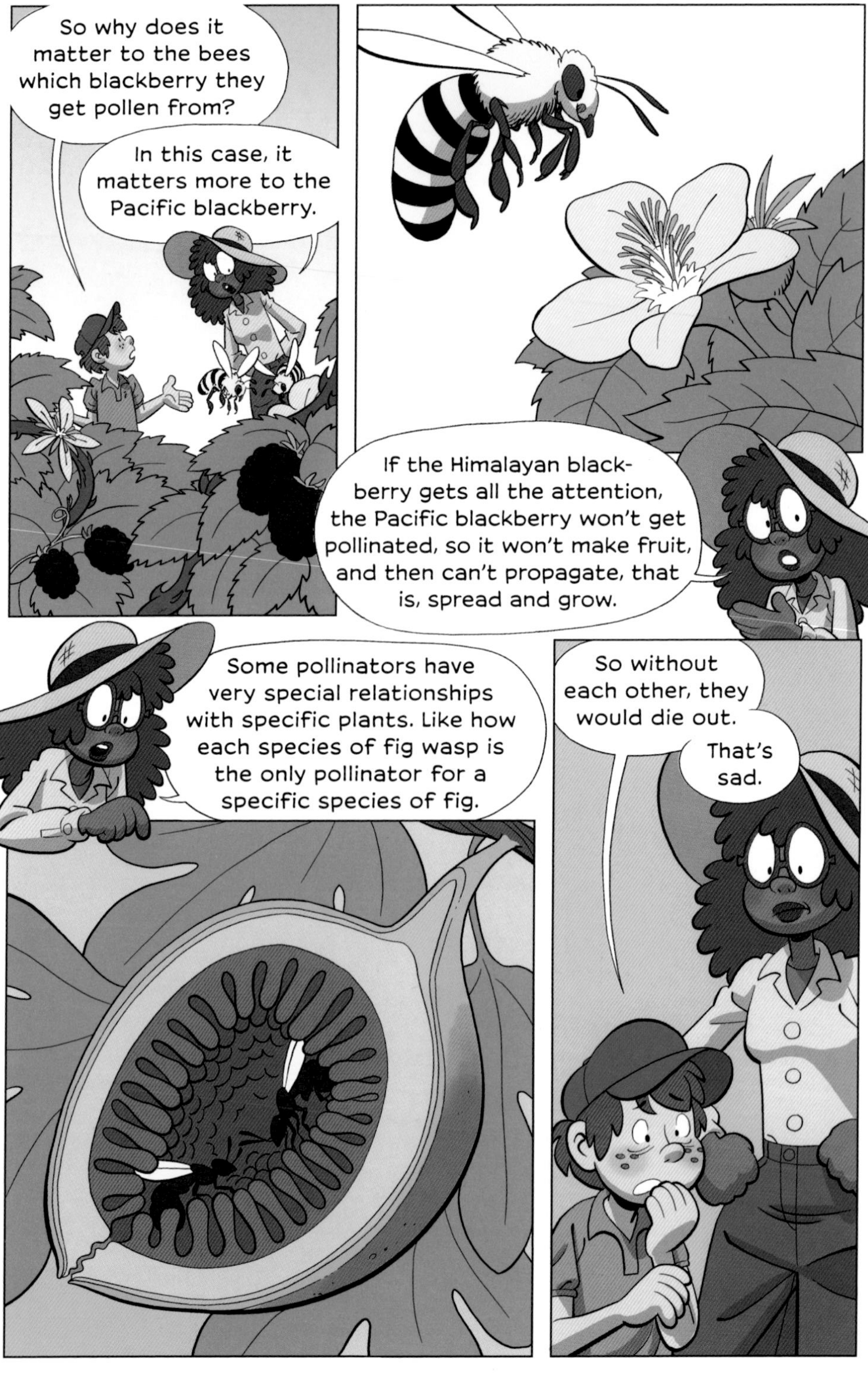

So why does it matter to the bees which blackberry they get pollen from?
In this case, it matters more to the Pacific blackberry.
If the Himalayan black-berry gets all the attention, the Pacific blackberry won't get pollinated, so it won't make fruit, and then can't propagate, that is, spread and grow.
Some pollinators have very special relationships with specific plants. Like how each species of fig wasp is the only pollinator for a specific species of fig.
So without each other, they would die out.
That's sad.

Without pollinators in general, many plants would die out. Which is why we need to be careful with things like pesticides.

Pesticides are indiscriminate poisons killing both the targeted pest insects and also the beneficial insects.

Pesticides are also mobile so they can travel through air, water, and soil to places we didn't mean to apply them.

Wow. It's rough out there for pollinators. Is there anything we can do to help them?

Of course!

So, Isaac. Are you allergic to bees?

No, fortunately. One kid in my class always has to have his EpiPen.

Then let's make a bee garden for your balcony!

Whoa, whoa.

I don't want a bunch of bees covering my balcony.

Oh no, they'll just nip in and out. We'll plant lots of flowers to feed the bees, and you'll have a lush garden to enjoy. Just leave the bees to their flowers. If one lifts a middle leg, you are upsetting it.

Growing a Bee Garden

white vinegar

organic soil

containers

If you have land to plant on, even better, but window boxes and potted plants work just as well.

1/8-inch nail (11 gauge) or so

plants

pebbles

horticultural charcoal

You can use seeds or starters from your local garden center— little plants already sprouted and grown. We'll use starters.

Soak your containers in distilled white vinegar (5 percent acidity) for 15 minutes to kill bacteria, then wash with hot water and a little soap, rinsing all the soap off. These can be cute planter pots or anything that will hold dirt: milk carton with the top cut off, yogurt container, or even an old shoe.

Select a variety of plants so something is blooming most of the year. Different species of bees come out of hibernation at different times. Most hibernate in the winter, so you want early spring through late fall blooms.

Ask your local garden center for native plants that bloom each season, but here are some places to start.

Spring

crocus · hyacinth · borage · calendula · wild lilac

Summer

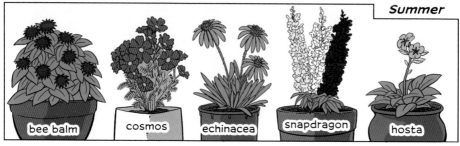

bee balm · cosmos · echinacea · snapdragon · hosta

Fall

zinnia · sedum · aster · witch hazel · goldenrod

If you're reusing a food container, use your nail to poke a few holes in the bottom so any excess water can drain out.

Put a layer of pebbles at the bottom of your pot, filling about one-fourth of the pot. This allows for excess water to drain more easily so the soil doesn't rot.

Put soil and your plant in. The top of the soil should be just below the top of the pot. You might need to put soil under the starter plant, and likely around the sides. Try to find soil without synthetic fertilizers.

After potting, a plant needs water to recover. This is a great time to use your rain barrel. You'll need to research how much water your specific plants need, but typically you water them a little every few days so the soil doesn't dry out. Too much water can make the roots rot.

Check with an adult if a tray or plate is needed to catch excess water that might leak out.

Place your potted plants out of the way where they won't fall or trip people. A balcony or porch is great for outdoor plants, though fire escapes are usually illegal. You'll have to research the plant to find out how much sun it needs. Some plants want sun all day, and others prefer shade. Some should also be brought inside before the first frost.

Now it's time to care for your garden. First, don't use pesticides, including insecticidal soaps. These can harm the bees you're trying to help. Instead, use natural defenses.

To discourage snails and slugs, crush up eggshells and place them around the pot edges.

If you find aphids (they love roses), plant these flowers. They'll attract ladybugs, who eat aphids.

angelica, calendula, caraway, chives*, cilantro*, cosmos, dill*, fennel*, feverfew, marigold, statice, sweet alyssum, yarrow

* These follow permaculture because you can also eat them!

93

You can also help weary bees by making a bee bar.

STOCKING A BEE BAR

Fill a shallow container with pebbles and twigs. These are basically the bar stools so the bees won't fall in the water when they come to drink.

Fill the container with water (use your rain barrel). Remember, there should be dry islands of pebbles and sticks for the bees to land on.

Now keep the container full at all times and always leave it in the same place. The bees learn that this is a consistent and safe place to get water. Remember, the water evaporates more quickly on hot days. If the water gets gross, you can empty and refill the bee bar.

If you find a bee who is sleeping, too tired to move on, you can help them get their energy back. Like this little lady.

See how we can walk up to her and she doesn't move?

Just a few twitches?

Mix two tablespoons of white granulated sugar with one tablespoon water. More water and the bee could drown in it.

Place the mixture on a spoon or plate next to the bee. The bee will crawl over, sip on their energy drink, and then take off!

What about honey? Can't I just feed them that?

Actually you shouldn't give them honey. Not only do they not want honey that's not from their hive, but it could make them sick.

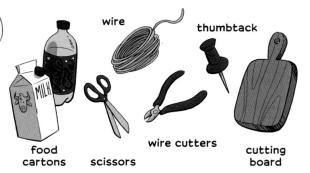

Upcycling Food Cartons as Flower Pots

And look at that, we have a garden on wheels!

Not for long.

These are going on my balcony.

wire

thumbtack

food cartons

scissors

wire cutters

cutting board

We'll use wire to hang old food cartons from the railing so you don't lose room on your balcony. This is 1 mm jewelry wire, but most wire works if it holds its shape when you bend it. The repurposed pots can be paper or plastic milk cartons or empty lotion bottles! Just make sure to clean them really well.

Cut the top off your carton. You can cut it straight across or get fancy and cut it at an angle or even a wavy line.

For a rectangular carton, rest it on a cutting board, and use your thumbtack to poke eight holes, two on each side of the corners (or evenly spaced pairs if it's a circle). A hammer and nail works, too.

Thread your wire in and out of each pair of holes. The wire will mostly be on the outside of the container.

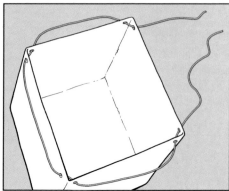

Leave about a foot of wire hanging out of the first and last holes. Cut it with wire cutters if it's too long.

Wind the wire around the railing of your balcony, then twist the ends of the wire together as a knot. You can place a pot in the carton or plant straight in the carton.

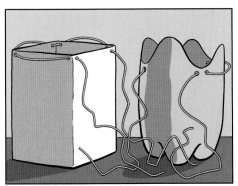

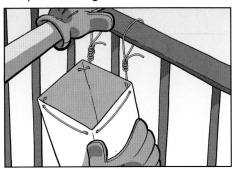

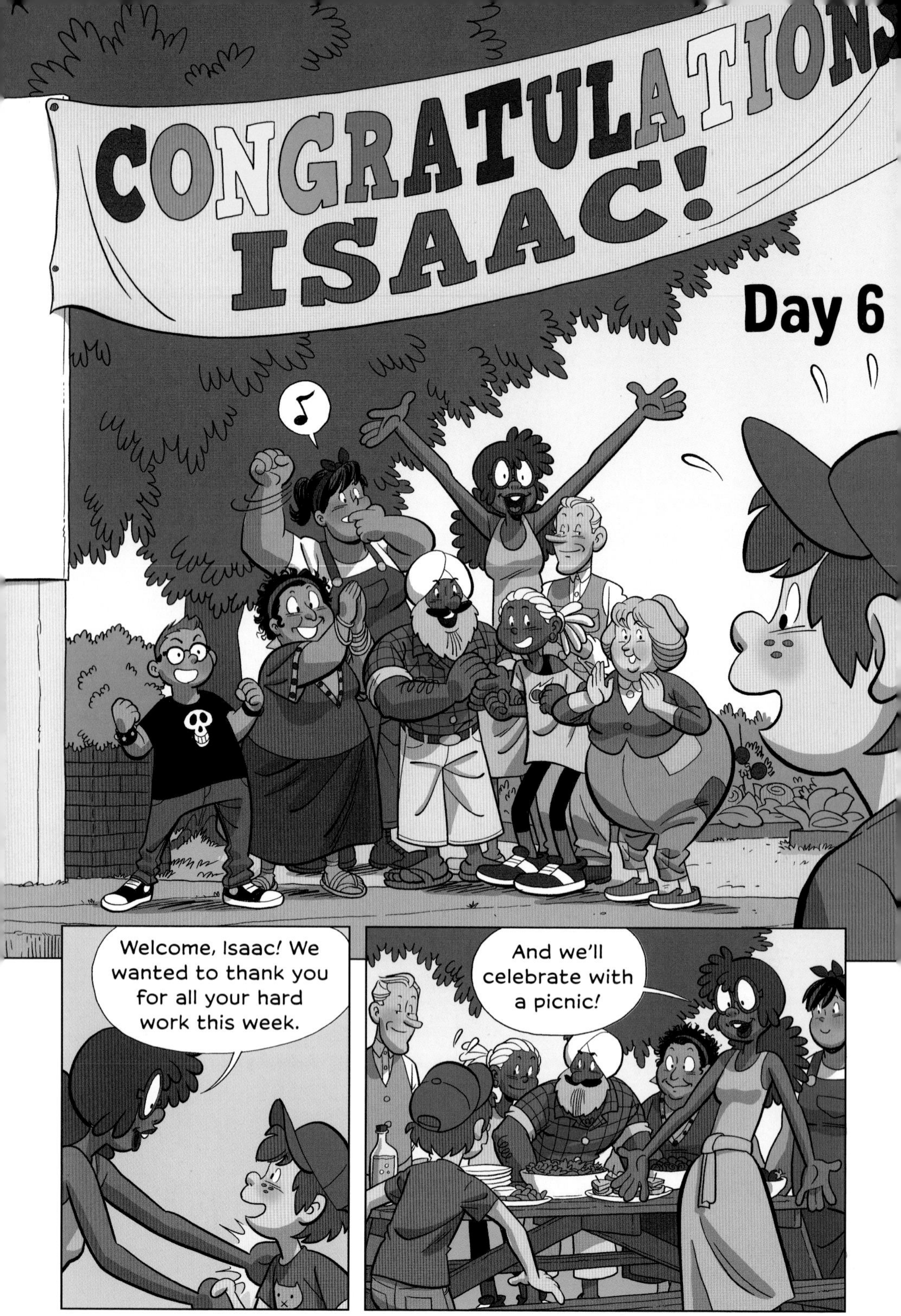
CONGRATULATIONS ISAAC!
Day 6
Welcome, Isaac! We wanted to thank you for all your hard work this week.
And we'll celebrate with a picnic!

These are cucumber sandwiches from my garden.

I made artichoke dip. Delicious.

Can't go wrong with artichokes.

Here's some stir-fry with peas from my garden, kale from Fin's garden, and spinach from Garet's garden.

Here's some braised Brussels sprouts.

I have some strawberries. That's it. I just plucked them.

There is so much food here. And you made it all?

Well, we grew as much as we could. But some things...

...we bought from local vendors.

Like bread and cream cheese!

Since transportation is a major source of pollution, the less distance your food travels, the less pollution created to move and refrigerate it. That applies to any product you buy.

Most cities have a *farmer's market* each week, at least from mid-spring to mid-autumn.

That's where I usually am on Saturdays, selling the produce we grow at my farm, Turnip the Beet.

There's no meat here.

Though most of us do eat meat, we don't eat it every day. Meat production can create a lot of pollution. So when we do eat meat, we go for "happy" meat, from farms where animals are treated and fed well without a lot of hormones and unnecessary antibiotics.

A farmer's market is typically one day a week at the same location, indoors or out.

It can be a small market with a handful of vendors, up to a large market with dozens of vendors.

You can typically find a website listing your local markets.

We bring our goods straight from the farm to sell to you and your family.

One of my favorite parts is that we can talk directly with consumers about our process of growing vegetables.

Plus, when you shop at the farmer's market, you are getting the freshest, most in-season produce.

For some of us, we are trying to have a lower *carbon footprint,* which just refers to the amount of greenhouse gases—carbon dioxide and methane—emitted through fossil fuel consumption for all the items we use.

Everything we use travels to us, unless we grow it or make it at home. But even the supplies, such as seeds or cloth, often travel to us.

And for each leg of the journey, there's a vehicle giving off carbon dioxide: airplanes, ships, trucks.

So the closer an item is to start off, the smaller the carbon footprint.

Correct!

It's so easy to travel now. For you, me, and anything we want to buy!

But all that travel has an impact. Most cars, buses, boats, and airplanes all give off carbon dioxide.

It's important to pay attention to how you travel, too.

So it's good that I walk to school or take an electric bus.

Right. And the items we buy often travel in similar ways to us. Instead of a bus, items are driven across the country in trucks. And more distant items travel in shipping containers on boats.

I can't tell where my shoes were made.

Have you noticed, in the winter and spring, you'll often get apples at the grocery that say they are from New Zealand?

Wow, no!

Those apples have traveled farther than I ever have.

Ha-ha! Yeah. We swap apples with the southern hemisphere because their winter is our summer and vice versa. It's great that we have fruit all year, but the carbon footprint of those apples is pretty high after traveling thousands of miles.

Lots of farms, including ours, have a CSA program. "CSA" stands for "community-supported agriculture," and is basically a subscription to their products, be it meat, dairy, vegetables, grains, legumes, or fish.

For our CSA, people can pick up their share each week at the farmer's market or at the farm on Wednesdays. Lots of farms offer multiple pickup locations. Some even deliver!

Most fruit and vegetables in stores have traveled anywhere from 1,500 to 2,500 miles.

If you shop at a farmer's market or join a CSA, you will be getting fresh food that has traveled less than 100 miles.

Some grocery stores label where local produce came from. This helps you pick the specific farms that you know are *sustainable* and *organic.*

So if I pick organic fruit from a local farm, it will be sustainable?

Not necessarily.

Sustainable means the farm uses sustainable practices.

The main goal for nearly any farm is to produce and sell enough food or fiber to support the farm's operation.

Which means they have long-term goals for their farm.

Sustainable farms also improve the environment through regenerating the soil in their fields, which aids the local flora and fauna.

They use resources efficiently, both non-renewable (such as gasoline) and renewable (such as solar power or rainwater).

And they try to enhance the quality of life on the farm and in society.

ORGANIC

SUSTAINABLE

Organic is completely separate from sustainable. Organic means farmers don't use synthetic pesticides or fertilizers. But they can still use organic pesticides and fertilizers.

Organic farms also can't use **GMOs**—genetically modified organisms.

These are plants that have had their genes edited in a lab.

* Cotton and corn are two of the most commonly genetically modified plants.

You **can** do all that without being sustainable.

Instead of GMOs, you can raise specific variations of vegetables and animals: cultivation for plants and selective breeding for animals.

Sustainability isn't just about growing things. There's also food packaging. That's another benefit at the farmer's market—often much less packaging. That's something to pay attention to for everything you buy.

When I got my phone, it was in three layers of plastic inside a box that was inside another box. It took me as long to get the phone out as it did to log in the first time.

Exactly.

You also have to watch out for single-use items, such as straws, plastic forks, and to-go containers. If you have to buy or use them, check the labels. Are you choosing something compostable, or at least recyclable?

Our favorite restaurant gives us a separate foam container for each part of the meal.

Polystyrene, the material in those foam containers, is made from fossil fuels and doesn't break down. Unfortunately, it's also really cheap to make and to ship, so lots of businesses use them.

But there are alternatives. Lots of restaurants use paper to-go containers. Some companies are replacing product packaging with custom-molded mycelium, made from fungal roots. The ultimate in composting.

We can't stop eating at that restaurant.

It's too delicious.

What can we do?

Local laws have started to ban non-sustainable, single-use items: plastic bags, foam containers, straws. But you can bring your own containers. Keep food containers or mason jars in your backpack. Some are even collapsible.

You can carry all sorts of reusable items with you. Let's all make some to-go packs!

I have everything we need in my car. I'll be right back.

What's a to-go pack?

It is a kit to carry with you so you can avoid single-use items.

Stocking a To-Go Kit

Alright, I'm back. We can make kits that have a:

reusable straw
so you don't have to use the plastic ones.

collapsible food container
so you don't need a doggie bag.

reusable water bottle
so you can bring your own fresh water and refill as needed.

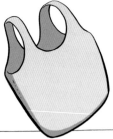

tote bag
so you don't need a bag when you buy something at the store. It can also hold the rest of your kit.

cutlery pack
to use instead of plastic flatware.

to-go mug
for your coffee or tea, which could also be collapsible.

cloth napkin
to avoid using paper napkins.

Some of these things you will have to buy, but with a little searching, you can find a shop in your area that carries them or buy them online if none are nearby.

Making a Tote Bag

T-shirt you don't
wear anymore

scissors

needle and thread
(optional)

ribbon or twine
(optional)

Let's
start with the
tote bag.

Everyone,
pick out
a T-shirt!

First we cut off the sleeves. You
can keep them for headbands! I use
them when washing my face.

Cut off the neck area
in a half circle.

For the bottom, you can either sew it or make fringe.

If you are sewing it, turn it inside out.

Lay your T-shirt flat. Thread your needle and pull the two ends together so the needle's at the halfway point. Tie a knot at the end.

Easy knot: wrap the end of the thread around your finger three times; pinching your thumb and forefinger together, roll the thread to your fingertip; pinching the full loop, pull the main thread tight.

At one edge, push the needle through both sides of fabric, right through the middle of the hem. Push it back through about 1/8 inch over and gently pull it all the way through, without bunching the fabric. Continue across in a straight line.

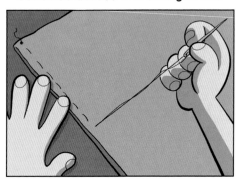

When you get to the end, make a loop and pull the thread through it to tie a knot against the fabric. Do this one or two more times. Cut.

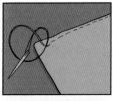

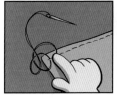

You can now turn it right-side out. ***Done!***

Alternatively, you can make a no-sew tote with fringe.

Across the bottom hem, cut 2–3 inches up at one-inch intervals through both sides. You don't have to be super precise here. Be careful not to cut off any fringe or you'll end up with a hole in the bottom of the bag.

Tie each of the front and back pairs together using double knots.

Lay your T-shirt flat.

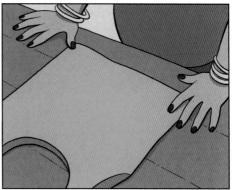

At the sides of the shirt, cut the side fringes along the fold so they are two pieces of fabric.

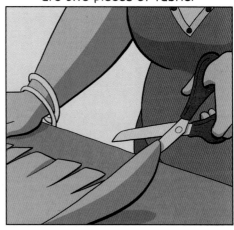

Ta-da!

You can also fold your tote into a small package if you want to keep it in your backpack or as a backup in another tote.

Sew the middle point of a ribbon or twine, about a foot long, to either the top or bottom of the handle.

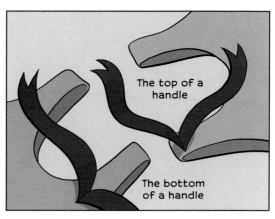

The top of a handle

The bottom of a handle

Tie it in a bow or tuck it into the bag.

Fold your tote up and it fits anywhere!

Making a Cutlery Pack

Now let's make cutlery packs!

pencil

pins

cloth napkin

needle and thread

cutlery you like to use (fork, spoon, butter knife, chopsticks, reusable straw). They should be no more than half the length of your napkin.

ribbon (optional)

You can get many of these items for cheap at a thrift store. Or ask an adult if you can use some from home!

Lay your silverware neatly on the middle of your napkin with a gap of at least half an inch between each item.

Fold the napkin up about a third and pin the napkin in place.

Using a pencil, make a straight line halfway between each item.

Remove the silverware and, using a needle and thread, sew along your marks. Use only a few feet of thread at a time so it doesn't get tangled.*

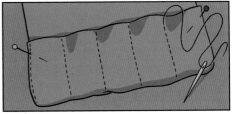

* Or use a sewing machine with the help of an adult.

Remove the pins and cut a piece of ribbon or twine about 1.5 feet long. Sew the mid-point of the ribbon or twine to the left side of the napkin, about halfway along the length of your silverware.

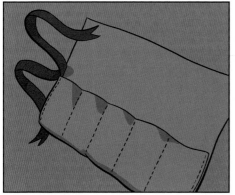

Place your silverware in the little pouches.

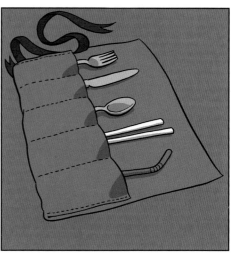

Fold the top part of the fabric down to hold your cutlery in place.

Starting from the right side, roll the pack up. Then wrap the ribbon around and tie a bow.

And you can use the napkin instead of paper napkins!

Thanks, Aurora! I learned a lot this week.

And I'm sorry I defaced your sign. But I am also a little glad I did, 'cause otherwise I wouldn't have met you!

I think I'm going to keep volunteering.

Great! I look forward to seeing you around. We have a lot more work for you, like that blank wall at the end of the garden.

Really?!

I think I see more paint in your future.

Awesome! I have so many ideas! Like a lot of rabbits.

Ha ha ha!

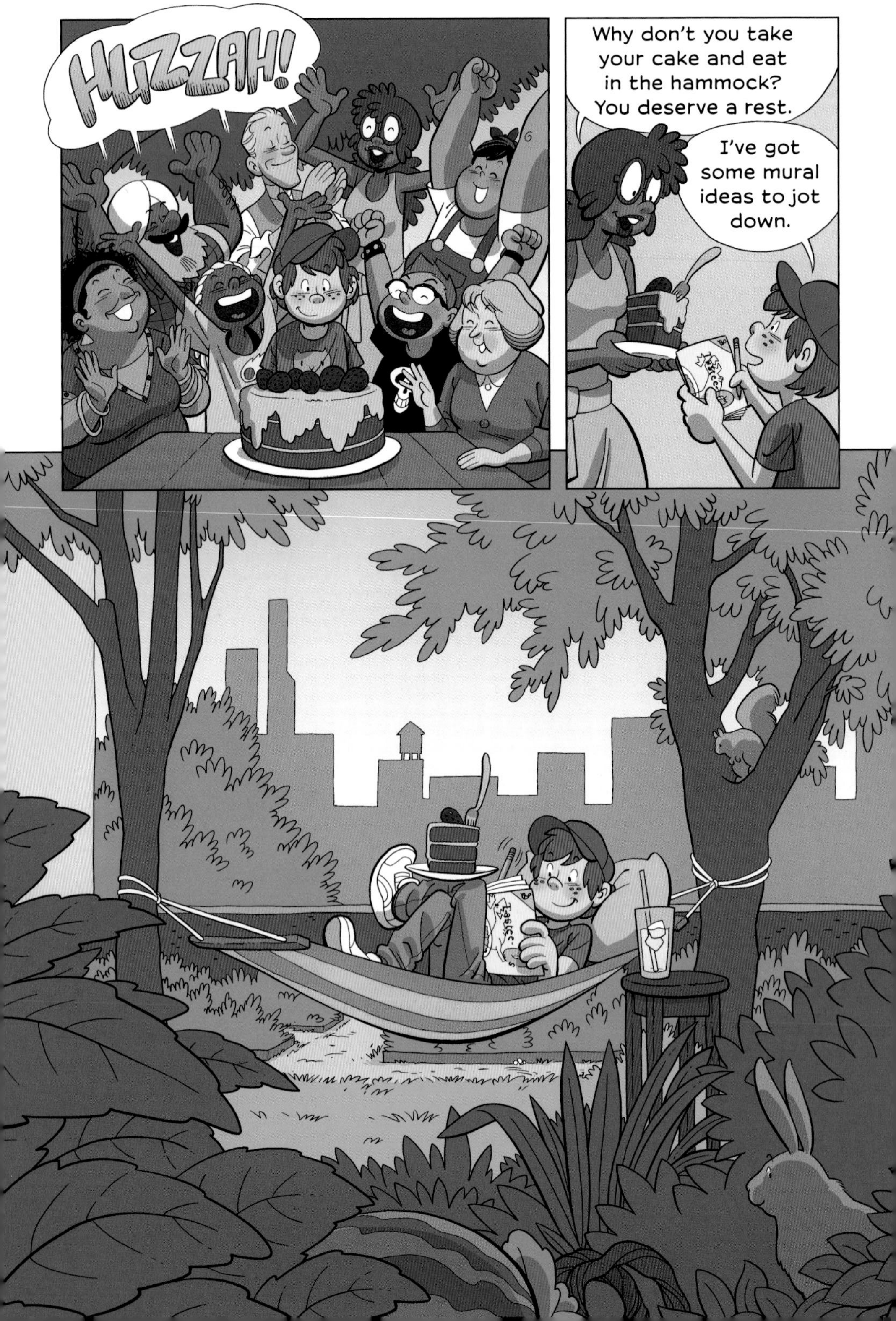
HUZZAH!
Why don't you take your cake and eat in the hammock? You deserve a rest.
I've got some mural ideas to jot down.

Glossary

basic need: what we need to live: food, water, air, safety, shelter, warmth, health

biodiversity: the variety of life in an ecosystem

carbon footprint: amount of carbon dioxide and other carbon compounds emitted by a person from the use of fossil fuels

closed system: a system that does not allow transfers in or out of itself

coevolution: influence of species on one another in their evolution, becoming interdependent

compostable: capable of disintegrating into natural elements, leaving no toxicity

ecosystem: community of living things and their environment

farmer's market: food market where local farmers sell directly to consumers

GMO: genetically modified organism, organism whose genetics have been altered through genetic engineering techniques

keystone species: a species that an ecosystem depends on so much that if it is removed (or added) it would drastically change the ecosystem

mycorrhizae: fungus that grows in harmony (though sometimes harmfully) with the roots of plants

organic: food or farming methods that don't use chemical fertilizers or pesticides

permaculture: development of agricultural ecosystems that are sustainable and self-sufficient

pesticide: substance for destroying insects or other pests harmful to a plant or animal

pollinator: animal that moves pollen from flower to flower

rain barrel: tank used to collect and store rainwater, typically from rooftops

renewable: not depleted when used

sustainability: ability to be maintained; avoids depleting a natural resource

waste: material that is not used or is a by-product of something

Easy Everyday Sustainability

Ride your bike or walk. (Reduce)

Use only the lights you need. (Reduce)

Use a sweater before the heater. (Reduce)

Turn off the faucet when brushing your teeth. (Reduce)

Cut one minute from your shower and avoid baths. (Reduce)

Donate used clothing, toys, and electronics. (Reuse)

Bring cutlery with you. (Reuse)

Recycle!

More Books about Sustainability!

World without Fish by Mark Kurlansky and Frank Stockton (Workman, 2011)

Eco Kids Self-Sufficiency Handbook by Alan Bridgewater (New Holland, 2009)

The New 50 Simple Things Kids Can Do to Save the Earth by Earthworks Group (Andrews McMeel Publishing, 2009)

The Big Green Book of the Big Blue Sea by Helaine Becker and Willow Dawson (Kids Can Press, 2012)

The Green Teen: The Eco-friendly Teen's Guide to Saving the Planet by Jenn Savedge (New Society Publishers, 2009)

There are many books about sustainability, but here are some of my favorites!

Next Steps to Promote Sustainability

Volunteer!

Community garden, composting, litter pickup, clothing swap, fabric recycling.

Join or start a sustainability club.

Adopt a park or road that you can help maintain.

Join a movement, such as Fridays for Future.

Start a zero-waste club at your school, helping the cafeteria and breakfast program move away from disposable products and encouraging students to bring waste-free lunches.

Prepare to become an informed voter.

Learn about local initiatives and laws to promote sustainability.

Have foam containers been banned from your municipality? Have plastic shopping bags?

What are the laws and regulations that encourage commuting via bicycle or public transit?

Be an environmental activist.

Attend workshops and lectures about how to take action on behalf of the environment, like those through Youth for Environmental Sanity (YES).

Learn about your local wildlife and how to help protect them, then work with your community to enact change.

What Are Other Kids Doing?

Greta Thunberg (Sweden) started when she was fifteen by holding up a sign outside the Swedish parliament that read "School strike for climate." From this simple act, other students engaged in protests within their own communities, and Fridays for Future was born. You can read more about her work in the book collecting her speeches, *No One Is Too Small to Make a Difference.*

Isra Hirsi (United States) cofounded US Youth Climate Strike and is now its coexecutive, leading student climate strikes. She was inspired by the Flint water crisis.

Jamie Margolin (United States) founded Zero Hour at seventeen, a movement to support new young activists and organizers with tools, training, and other resources.

Kallan Benson (United States) is the fourteen-year-old national coordinator for Fridays for Future USA and codirects Parachutes for the Planet, which encourages people to express their concerns about the future through community art.

Leah Namugerwa (Uganda) has begun a petition to get the Ugandan government to ban plastic bags. She started in Fridays for Future Uganda at fourteen, despite her government's harsh response to strikers.

Lilly Platt (The Netherlands) has been working to end the use of plastic since she was very young. She is now a Youth Ambassador for the Plastic Pollution Coalition and a Child Ambassador for HOW Global and World Cleanup Day.

First Second

Published by First Second
First Second is an imprint of Roaring Brook Press,
a division of Holtzbrinck Publishing Holdings Limited Partnership
120 Broadway, New York, NY 10271
firstsecondbooks.com
mackids.com

All instructions included in this book are provided as a resource for parents and children.
While all due care has been taken, we recommend that an adult supervise children at all times when following
the instructions in this book. The projects in this book are not recommended for children three years and under
due to potential choking hazard. Neither the authors nor the publisher accept any responsibility for any loss,
injury, or damages sustained by anyone resulting from the instructions contained in this book.

Library of Congress Control Number: 2021916343

Our books may be purchased in bulk for promotional, educational, or business use.
Please contact your local bookseller or the Macmillan Corporate and Premium Sales Department
at (800) 221-7945 ext. 5442 or by email at MacmillanSpecialMarkets@macmillan.com.

First edition, 2022
Edited by Robyn Chapman and Alison Wilgus
Cover and interior book design by Molly Johanson
Flatter: Crystal Nehler
Sustainability consultant: Katherine Martinko

Printed in China by 1010 Printing International Limited, Kwun Tong, Hong Kong

ISBN 978-1-250-62064-4 (paperback)
1 3 5 7 9 10 8 6 4 2

ISBN 978-1-250-62063-7 (hardcover)
1 3 5 7 9 10 8 6 4 2

Pencilled and inked digitally using custom brushes in Clip Studio Paint EX
and colored in Photoshop, using a Cintiq 27QHD with a Mac Mini.

Don't miss your next favorite book from First Second!
For the latest updates go to firstsecondnewsletter.com and sign up for our enewsletter.

Angela Boyle is a natural science illustrator and cartoonist from Bellingham, Washington. She received an MFA from The Center for Cartoon Studies in 2016. She runs the natural science comic anthology series Awesome 'Possum, with four volumes so far. The Brazilian tapir is her favorite animal, only partly because it has a mohawk. Angelabcomics.com

Les McClaine is the Eisner-nominated author of Jonny Crossbones, Life With Leslie, *Repeat Until Death*, and *Highway 13*. He has also illustrated numerous comics including The Tick and The Middleman. His other illustration credits include *Tune: Still Life*, *Head Games: The Graphic Novel,* and *Old Souls*, all from First Second. Lesmcclaine.com